Wales

AA

MINI GUIDE

GW00492631

MENAI BRIDGE

Author: John Gillham
Managing Editor: Paul Mitchell
Art Editor: Carole Philp
Editor: Sandy Draper
Cartography provided by the Mapping Services Department of AA Publishing
Internal colour reproduction: Michael Moody

Produced by AA Publishing
© Automobile Association Developments Limited 2007

Published by AA Publishing (a trading name of Automobile Association Developments Limited,
whose registered office is Fanum House, Basing View, Basingstoke, Hampshire RG21 4EA; registered
number 1878835).

A03033F

TRADE ISBN-13: 978-0-7495-5590-0
SPECIAL ISBN-13: 978-0-7495-5697-6

A CIP catalogue record for this book is available from the British Library.

Visit AA Publishing's website www.theAA.com/travel

Colour reproduction by Keene Group, Andover.
Printed in China by Everbest.

CONTENTS

INTRODUCTION

There's something special about crossing the borders into Wales. Maybe, it is the way the flat fields of the English shires soar up into the Welsh hills, or those funny sounding, unpronounceable place names on the road signs. When I see the 'Croeso i Gymru' – Welcome to Wales – sign, my spirits lift, my pulse quickens and those mountains call. The landscape of Wales can compete with the best of anywhere in the British Isles. Its high, jagged mountains in the north are like a child's impression of what a mountain should look like. Its quiet valleys feel remote and undiscovered. In the south, the Pembrokeshire coastline juts its rugged teeth into the foaming sea and the emphatic crests of the Brecons soar and sweep above the wooded vales. Modern Wales has a buzz but it is still a land of dragons, of druidic landscapes, warriors and poetry.

Borderland Wales is fertile and verdant, with rolling foothills rising to high, heather moors. Pretty villages set deep into little-known valleys like the Ceiriog and the Tanat south of Llangollen.

The Conwy Valley marks the transition to the mountains of Wales: Snowdonia. Here the great Carneddau whalebacks decline to the sea, backed up by the distinctive craggy Glyderau range and Snowdon itself. All 15 of the 3,000-foot (915m) Welsh peaks lie in a compact region between Conwy, Caernarfon and Beddgelert. Villages at the foot of the mountains like Capel Curig, Betws-y-Coed and Llanberis are dedicated to walkers and climbers. But for those who don't climb, you're never far from the yawning sands of the coast, a narrow-gauge steam railways or one of the magnificent castles built by Edward I.

In absolute contrast to Snowdonia's alpine scenery, the moorland peaks and cwms of the Elenydd region of Mid Wales are simpler in form, with wild and remote upland plateaux opening out to big, big skies.

The great flat-topped sandstone escarpments of the Brecon Beacons mark the entry to South Wales, where rural landscapes descend deep into 'the valleys'. From the Industrial Revolution onwards, the valleys were the engine room of Wales. Coal, iron and steel fuelled an economy that led to massive growth in the ports of Cardiff, Swansea and Newport. After years the decline of these industries posed challenges but, remembering their maritime roots, the towns and cities have been revitalised. Cardiff's vibrant new bay area with its marinas, Millennium Centre and Senedd Building.

Wales meets the Atlantic Ocean at Pembrokeshire, whose spectacular coast is as rugged as anything Cornwall can offer. Unlike the West Country, Pembrokeshire can offer the coast without the crowds, and quaint fishing villages without those huge coach parks.

Great Ormes
Head
Holyhead
**ANGLESEY
& LLEYN
PENINSULA**
Holy
Island
Anglesey
A5025
A55
Bangor
Caernarfon
A55
A5
1085
Snowdon ▲
A487
Lleyn Peninsula
A497
Porthmadog
A470
**SNOWDONIA:
MOUNTAINS &
VALLEYS**
Conwy
Llandudno
A55
Rhyl
A548
Denbigh
A525
Mold
A494
A55
Betws-y-
Coed
A5
Bala
A494
Wrexham
A5
Llangollen
A483
A525
A495
A49
Liverpool
M53
M56 A49
Chester
A41
A525
**NORTHEAST
WALES &
MARCHES**
A5
A458

Barmouth
A496
A470
Dolgellau
A470
A493
Machynlleth
A458 Welshpool
A483
A470
A489
Shrewsbury
A458
A458

CARDIGAN
BAY

Aberystwyth
A44
A485
A470
A483
Llangurig
Rhayader
A44
Knighton
Llandrindod
Wells
A481
A489
ENGLAND
A49

Aberaeron
A487
A482
**BRECON BEACONS
& MID WALES**
Lampeter
A483
A470
Hay-on-Wye
A438
Hereford
A465
A49

Strumble
Head
Cardigan
A487
A484
A485
A40
Llandovery
Llandeilo
A40
Brecon Beacons
Brecon
A470
A479
Abergavenny
A465
Monmouth
A466
A40
A44

Fishguard
PEMBROKESHIRE
St David's
A40
A478
Carmarthen
A40
A48
A483
A4067
Merthyr
Tydfil
A465
A4042
A449
Chepstow
M48

Haverfordwest
A4076
A40
Llanelli
M4
**GOWER PENINSULA
& COAST**
Cwmbran
M4

Pembroke
A477
Swansea
Gower
Neath
Caerphilly
Newport
M4

Bridgend
M4
A48
Cardiff
Bristol
A38

ESSENTIAL SPOTS

Visit Cardiff Castle and enjoy a wealth of culture and good shopping...gaze across the majestic Brecon Beacons...experienced walkers can get up very high in the Snowdonia National Park...walk along the coast at Pembrokeshire or enjoy the views on the spectacular Gower Peninsula... explore the vast expanse of Fforest Fawr and the Black Mountains...discover waterfall country...visit Edward I's castles at Carnaerfon, Conwy or Laugharne...visit Machynlleth for an alternative view on modern living...take a ride on the Brecon Mountain Railway...visit the charming border town of Chepstow or walk along part of Offa's Dyke...admire Thomas Telford's feat of bridge engineering across the Menai Strait or the Victorian dam of Craig Goch Reservoir, which holds back the waters of the Elan Valley...discover the mysteries of Preseli and St David's or the harbour at Milford Haven.

1

1 Offa's Dyke

This important boundary ditch and embankment was built in the 8th century by the Mercian king Offa to divide England and Wales. It runs from Prestatyn in the north to Sedbury near Chepstow in the south.

2 Criccieth Castle

Built around 1230 for Llywelyn the Great, this superb castle stands on a headland above the lovely seaside town of Criccieth.

3 Bala Lake Railway

Steam coaches, which once worked in the slate quarries of North Wales, are now put to use hauling passenger coaches from the Llanuwchyllyn station along the lake to Bala.

4

4 Portmeirion
Welsh architect Sir Clough Williams-Ellis built his fairy-tale Italianate village on a peninsula on the shores of Cardigan Bay.

5 Cardiff Quay
The city's revamped Cardiff Bay waterfront area offers plenty of shops, bars, restaurants and visitor attractions, including the Wales Millennium Centre, a showpiece arts centre for Welsh culture.

5

6 Menai Strait

Thomas Telford's fine suspension bridge of 1826 strides gracefully across the Menai Strait, linking ancient Anglesey with the Welsh mainland.

7 Conwy Castle

The imposing entrance to Edward I's 13th-century castle dominates the town. The castle forms part of Conwy's original system of defence, which includes the town walls.

Day One in Wales

For many people a weekend break or a long weekend is a popular way of spending their leisure time. These pages offer a loosely planned itinerary designed to ensure that you make the most of your time, whatever the weather, and see and enjoy the very best of Wales. The first day seeks out Monmouthshire's medieval history, visiting an abbey, four castles and an ancient gated bridge. It illustrates perfectly the beauty of Wales' southern border area.

Friday Night

Make your way to the border town of Chepstow. If there's time, take a walk around its pretty streets and ginnels to see the 13th-century town walls and the imposing Norman castle, which is set high on cliffs overlooking the River Wye. The Castle View Inn is the perfect choice for a relaxing start to the weekend, with fine food and accommodation.

Saturday Morning

It's well worth taking a closer look at Chepstow Castle. Now run by CADW, the castle's construction in stone began in the same year as the Battle of Hastings. The A466 to the west of the town takes the route through the beautiful Wye Valley. Visit the 12th-century Cistercian priory at Tintern. Though roofless, the abbey is still one of the most elegant ecclesiastical buildings in Wales.

LLANTHONY PRIORY

Saturday Lunch

Take a leisurely lunch at the Abbey Hotel in Tintern, where you can relax in the front garden, which also happens to be the priory grounds.

Saturday Afternoon

The Wye meets the Monnow River at historic Monmouth, birthplace of King Henry V and Charles Rolls of Rolls-Royce fame – their statues are in Agincourt Square. Don't miss the impressive 13th-century Monnow Bridge, the only one in Britain to have a fortified gatehouse.

Follow lanes out of town to Skenfrith, which lies among green rolling hills several miles to the northwest. The castle (free entry) is idyllically set on a green by the banks of the Monnow – wonderful for picnics. More lanes lead westwards to White Castle, a fine moated 12th-century fortress.

Now head for Llanfihangel Crucorney, before following narrow lanes that wind through the stunningly beautiful Vale of Ewyas, which cuts through the Black Mountains. Half way along is Llanthony Priory (free entry), which surprisingly has it's own pub beneath the arches.

Saturday Night

The Gospel Pass at the head of the Vale of Ewyas has superb long-distance views and is an ideal place to stop and stretch your legs. Descend to the literary town of Hay-on-Wye, where Kilverts offers good, comfortable accommodation and tasty meals in the bar or restaurant.

Day Two in Wales

Our second and final day offers the chance to explore the
Brecon Beacons National Park. After a relaxing start, the day
gets going with a drive to Llangorse for lunch and a visit to
the lake. In the afternoon there's an opportunity for a walk
on a clearly defined path or you can take a ride on the Brecon
Mountain Railway, one of Wales' great little steam railways.

Sunday Morning

Hay-on-Wye is a fascinating little market town. On Sunday morning, you'll find the town ticks over at a more leisurely pace. If the weather is fine and dry there is apicturesque stroll by the river, which follows the Wye Valley Walk route westwards along the north bank. Many of the town's antiquarian bookshops open around mid-morning.

Head southwest out of the town, passing through Talgarth before taking the B4560 to Llangorse, a small village sheltering in the verdant lake-filled basin that is squeezed between the Black Mountains and the Brecon Beacons.

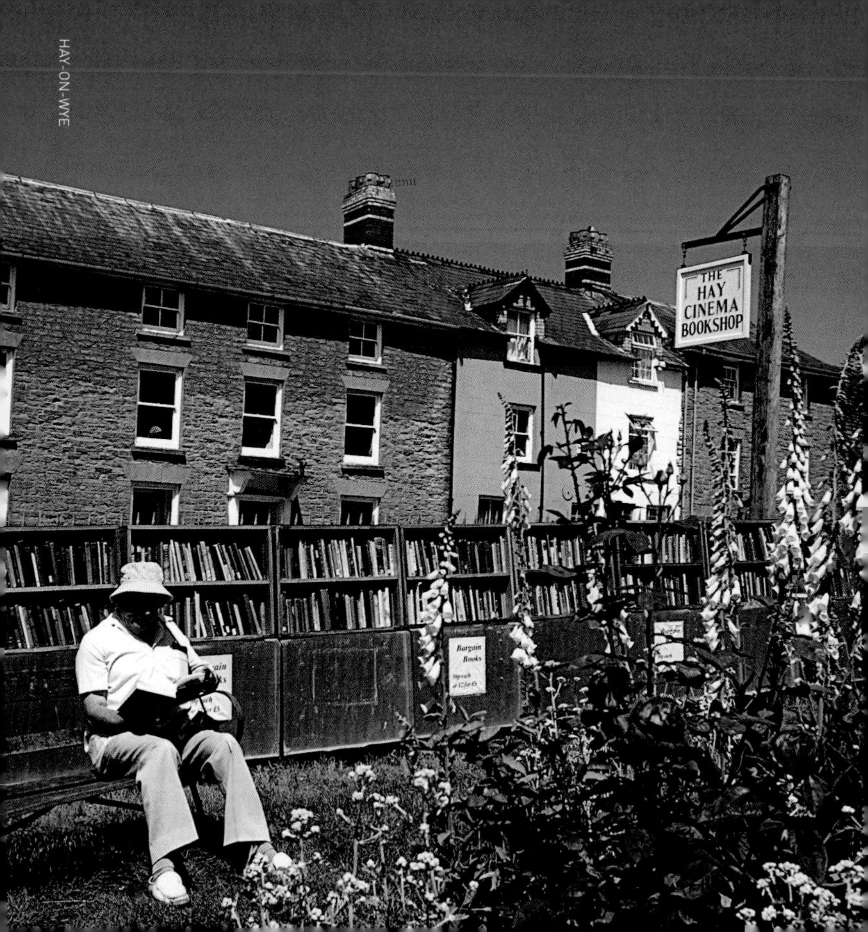
THE
HAY
CINEMA
BOOKSHOP
Bargain
Books

BRECON BEACONS NATIONAL PARK

Sunday Lunch

Take lunch at the Red Lion at Llangorse and if there's time drive down to the lake, which has a lovely view across to the Brecons and is good for birding.

Sunday Afternoon

After heading south to the A40, head for Talybont-on-Usk, where quiet country lanes track alongside the lovely Talybont Reservoir and up to a high pass to the south of the main Brecon Beacons ridge. If it's fine, you have some walking boots, a map and three hours to spare, the clearly defined there-and-back path is well worth doing.

The lane descends into the afforested valley of the Taf Fechan, past the Pentwyn Reservoir into Pontsticill village, where a right turn leads to Pant Station on the Brecon Mountain Railway. If you didn't do the walk, there should be plenty of time for a return trip on the narrow-gauge steam railway (it takes just over an hour). There's a licensed restaurant and children's play area by the station, so this is a good spot for supper before returning home.

Anglesey &
Lleyn Peninsula

INTRODUCTION

The Menai Strait, between the castle-crowned towns of Beaumaris and Caernarfon, has always set Anglesey apart from its Welsh neighbours. Its dolmen-dotted interior is fringed by a coastline of steep cliffs and sandy bays. Over on the mainland, the narrow coastal plains rear up to the cloud-capped foothills of Snowdonia. Separated by a mere sliver of water, it's not surprising that Anglesey and the Lleyn Peninsula have so much in common.

Unmissable attractions

Visit Aberdaron, picture-postcard pretty and filled with whitewashed cottages, and a wide sand-and-pebble beach popular with watersports enthusiasts...take a walk along the coast and spot the colonies of sea birds at South Stack...gaze across the moat to Beaumaris Castle, perhaps the most beautiful of Edward I's castles or Caernarfon, the most ambitious, intended to be the seat of government and the monarch's official residence... explore the wildlife habitat at Newborough Warren, a National Nature Reserve, which covers 1,500 acres (607ha) of shifting sand dunes and forest plantations...enjoy the hydrangeas that blossom in the mild climate at Plas Newydd, on the banks of the Menai Strait.

1

2

1 South Stack Lighthouse
Located near Holyhead on Anglesey, South Stack Lighthouse Visitor Centre is reached via a flight of steps to a suspension bridge.

2 Beaumaris
One of Edward I's most complete and romantic castles, Beaumaris was built to guard the approach to the Menai Strait and Anglesey.

3 Porthmadog
A harbour town, on the Glaslyn Estuary, Porthmadog is a popular holiday spot with a beautiful beach.

4 Caernarfon Castle
Imposing and stately, Caernarfon Castle is the most impressive of Edward I's fortifications.

4

5

ABERDARON & BARDSEY ISLAND

Aberdaron is often described as being the Land's End of North Wales. This is being kind to the, in my opinion, over-commercialised Land's End and unkind to Aberdaron. For this old fishing village, which lies at the mouth of the River Daron at the end of the Lleyn Peninsula, is chocolate-box pretty, with lovely whitewashed cottages gleaming against a backdrop of blue sea and golden cliffs and is steeped in the history of Celtic saints and pilgrims. Old Y Gegin Fawr café, in the centre of the village by the little stone bridge, dates from the 13th century, when it was used as a communal kitchen for the pilgrims on their way to Bardsey Island.

Aberdaron's wide sand and pebble beach is popular for fishing, watersports and bathing. At the end of September each year the beach hosts an open-air folk festival.

St Hywyn's Church, which is located right next to the beach, is in two halves, one dating back to 1137

Visit

NEWBOROUGH WARREN AND FOREST

Newborough Warren was created in the 13th century when wild storms submerged farmland beneath sand dunes. Rabbits were soon to colonise the area, hence its name Newborough Warren. To save the village of Newborough from further sand encroachment, Queen Elizabeth I made it an offence to cut down the dunes' natural vegetation, marram grass, which was used for mat-making. Later on, a pine forest was planted to offer further protection. Now a national nature reserve, the dunes and slacks of the area host many species of wild flowers including the marsh orchid and grass of Parnassus.

and the other, an extension, around 1400. The poet R S Thomas (1913–2000), a nominee for the Nobel Prize for Literature, was the local vicar here between 1954 and 1967 and the church contains interpretations of his life and works. The exposed position of the church has resulted in damage from the sea's proximity over the years, but it is now being restored to the glory days when it would have been the last stop for those many intrepid pilgrims, before they ventured across the wild – and sometimes – treacherous waters to Bardsey Island (Ynys Enlli).

Modern-day travellers can take a very enjoyable boat trip to Bardsey from Porth Meudwy, around the bay from Aberdaron. Sharp-eyed visitors often spot dolphins, porpoises and seals on the way across. They'll surely spot at least some of the island's 16,000 breeding pairs of Manx shearwaters. Bardsey, which is just over 2 miles (3km) long and rises to 548 feet (167m) at Mynydd Enlli, has been designated a National Nature Reserve.

Celtic monks settled here in the 6th century but only the tower remains of the 13th-century, Augustinian abbey. Many graves have been discovered on the island, giving rise to the claim that it is the resting place of 20,000 saints.

BEAUMARIS

These days the busy, non-stop A55 dual carriageway speeds most tourists on their way to Holyhead for the ferry-boat crossings to both Dublin and Dun Laoghaire in Ireland. Telford's graceful suspension bridge of 1824 now carries local traffic, but it is still a superb sight, enhanced by the dramatic backdrop of the peaks of Snowdonia's mountains.

After the busy village of Menai Bridge you'll find the small town of Beaumaris, which is dominated by its romantic-looking 13th-century castle. Edward I chose the site, which he said should be called *beau marais*, which means fair marsh.

Beaumaris Castle is regarded as one of the finest examples of Master James of St George's designs and wasn't finished due to lack of money and supplies. Although the walls never reached their intended height, the low-slung look is quite appealing and with the filled moat, four concentric layers of fortifications, a private sea dock and surrounded by

MENAI BRIDGE

peaceful parkland, it's most people's idea of a perfect castle.

Beaumaris town dates largely from the Victorian period, although the courthouse opposite the castle dates back to 1614. It is a major yachting centre – the Royal Anglesey Yacht Club resides here – and regular boat trips, for fishing or sightseeing, start from the pier.

Visit

THE WELSH HIGHLAND RAILWAY

By 2009 it is hoped that the dedicated engineers of the narrow-gauge Welsh Highland Railway will have finished building the line from Caernarfon to Porthmadog. In so doing, it will re-establish a connection that was closed in 1941. Today the little steam train makes a 12-mile (19km) journey from Caernarfon through the mountains to Rhyd Ddu, a small village at the foot of Snowdon, passing the beautiful lake Llyn Cwellyn en route. Special carriages allow the transportation of bicycles.

CAERNARFON

Dominated by its majestic 13-towered castle, Caernarfon guards the mouth of the Afon Seiont (Saint River) and the western end of the Menai Strait. The castle is the most imposing of Edward I's 'iron ring'. Begun in 1283 on the site of a motte-and-bailey castle, it would become a royal palace, designed to symbolise domination over the Welsh. It's an impressive sight with its mighty polygonal towers and ramparts that are remarkably intact. It is not surprising therefore that it was chosen by the Royal Family to be the setting for Prince Charles' investiture as Prince of Wales – some 700 years after Edward's son became the first English Prince of Wales in the same place. Caernarfon castle, now under the care of CADW, also houses the regimental Museum of the Royal Welsh Fusiliers.

Medieval walls with towered gates extend from the castle around the old town. The narrow streets are lined with many fascinating buildings. Some of these are Georgian and Victorian, but a few, including St Mary's Church built into those walls, are much older.

There is a town trail leaflet, available from the TIC, which will guide you from the Castle Square through the old gates, around the old red-light district of Northgate, where you'll see the 15th-century Black Boy Inn, the castle and the old Slate Quay. The trail shows that this was a seafaring town and the Maritime Museum on Bank Quay near Victoria Dock reinforces this, with a history of seafaring and industry in the area. Exhibits include models of ships, photographs and artefacts.

Caernarfon's long history predates the Normans by many centuries. The Romans, under the governance of Cnaeus Julius Agricola, conquered the Ordovices (an early Welsh tribe) in AD 77 and shortly afterwards established a fort, named, Segontium to the southeast of the present town. Like many Roman forts, Segontium had

Visit

CAERNARFON AIRWORLD AVIATION MUSEUM

Based at Caernarfon Airport, Dinas Dinlle tells the fascinating story of the RAF and the Mountain Rescue Service. It has plenty of genuine combat aircraft from the past to examine, including the Hawker Hunter, the Vampire and Javelin. You can also watch aviation footage in the small cinema.

defences of earth and timber, with gates and parallel streets. At the height of its strength it would have housed a thousand troops, all non-Roman citizens called cohorts. One such regiment known to have served here was called the First Cohort of Sunici, recruited from Germany. Coins discovered at archaeological digs show that the Romans occupied Segontium until about AD 394, a very long span, which indicates its strategic importance. The fine museum here exhibits and interprets artefacts from the Roman era.

41

HOLY ISLAND

While Holyhead is the largest of all of Anglesey's towns, with a good yachting marina, a maritime museum, a beach (Penrhos) and the island's highest hill, it's a rather unattractive place, little more than a busy transit port for Ireland since the Act of Union 1821. A far better base to discover Holy Island would be Trearddur Bay on the wild southwest coast. St Brigit is said to have landed here at the end of the 5th century and the little church is dedicated to her. Here the coastline is heavily indented with rocky promontories, low cliffs and islets enclosing small sandy beaches. In the central region there is one superb sweeping sandy cove overlooked by a local yacht club, the lifeboat station and the huge whitewashed building of the fine Trearddur Bay Hotel, which is right at the centre of all things local.

To the north of Trearddur the rough and rugged coastline becomes truly spectacular. The view from Ellins Tower, the RSPB information centre, to South Stack lighthouse is stunning. The cliffs of South Stack are a haven for flocks of seabirds including guillemots, skuas and gannets. When the wild west wind blows it's easy to see why Anglesey's perilous waters were the cause of so many terrible shipwrecks.

The limestone headland of Holyhead Mountain, just beyond South Stack, looks much higher than its mere 719-foot (220m) altitude would imply. Clad with heathland it is capped by a huge Celtic fort, Cae'r y Twr, built on the site of an older Roman watchtower.

MOELFRE & ANGLESEY'S COAST

More than any other village in Anglesey, Moelfre has a history of dramatic and daring lifeboat rescues. You can find out all about them at the Moelfre Seawatch Centre, which is sited not far from the harbour. Whitewashed fishermen's cottages are scattered on the headland overlooking a small harbour, a shingle beach and the

little island, Ynys Moelfre. There are wonderful clifftop paths to Dulas Bay, and in the opposite direction to Benllech and Red Wharf Bay.

Benllech is a modern-looking resort with a sandy beach and good facilities for visitors. Just a short walk south on the coastal path brings you to Red Wharf Bay where there's a huge expanse of sand, tidal mud and salt marshes – the sands stretch for 2.5 miles (4km) to Llandonna. The bay is superb for walking and birding: you'll more than likely spot redshanks, curlews, shelduck and oystercatchers. You'll also find Anglesey's best pub, The Ship Inn, and restaurant, the Old Boat House, are here.

NEFYN & LLEYN'S COAST
Nefyn, the largest of Lleyn's northern coastal villages, has two long sandy beaches. The one below the main village is beautifully situated, sheltered by vegetated shaly cliffs and has stunning views back along the gently arcing bay

to the mountains known as the Yr Eifl, (the Rivals). The view is slightly marred by a row of tatty sheds parading as beach huts. Porthdinllaen, the next cove beneath Morfa Nefyn, has the same shaly cliffs and a wonderful crescent-shaped sandy beach framed by a rocky promontory with an Iron Age fort on top. The Ty Coch pub here at

Visit

DIN LLIGWY – AN ANCIENT VILLAGE
Hidden in woodland, a mile (1.6km) or so inland from Moelfre, is a preserved Celtic settlement. The half-acre (0.2ha) site consists of foundations of a number of buildings, with the entire area enclosed by a thick double wall, built in the 4th-century AD, during the last years of the Roman Empire. In a nearby field are the remains of a neolithic burial chamber, the Lligwy tomb. This has a massive capstone weighing about 25 tons beneath which are buried the remains of 15 to 30 people, and pieces of beaker and grooved ware pottery.

Porthdinllaen has to be one of the best-sited pubs in Wales – it's right on the beach!

East of Nefyn the road turns inland to climb over the shoulders of Yr Eifl. Perched on the east summit of these granite mountains is Tre'r Ceiri, the 'town of giants' in legend but in reality, one of the best-preserved ancient forts in Wales. A gigantic Bronze Age burial cairn lies in the centre of an elaborate ancient settlement, where shattered stone walls enclose dozens of well-formed hut circle foundations. It's well worth taking the zig-zag roadside path through the heather to see them.

Lleyn's north coast gets more sparsely populated as you go west. This was largely the preserve of fishermen in days gone by – the locals still fish for crabs and lobsters – but the cliffs, coves and beaches are a real haven for holiday-makers looking for a little elbow room. Porth Iago has a tiny rock-bound beach – on a sunny day here you could be forgiven for thinking you were in Sardinia. Porth Oer, better known as Whistling Sands because the texture of the sand grains make them whistle underfoot, is a larger beach, backed by steep grassy cliffs, with safe bathing and a café.

PORTHMADOG & SOUTH LLEYN

Centred around a small harbour and the causeway William Madock built to reclaim land on the Glaslyn Estuary, Porthmadog is the most popular holiday resort in Lleyn. Many visitors come to ride on one of the two narrow-gauge railways, the Welsh Highland, which will eventually reach Caernarfon, and the Ffestiniog, which takes a scenic route to Blaenau Ffestiniog. A short walk leads past Porthmadog's boatyards and over a heavily wooded headland to reach the sheltered and pretty beach at Borth y Guest, where life is taken at a leisurely pace.

A few miles further east lies Criccieth, whose castle stands on a huge rhyolite crag that juts out into Tremadog Bay. It's part of Edward

I's 'iron ring' but, as there was already a Welsh castle on the spot, the English king only had to annexe and enlarge it. The twin-towered gatehouse was built by Llewelyn the Great in around 1240. The castle was left in its current ruinous state in 1404 after being captured by Welsh prince Owain Glyn Dwr. Despite its one-time strategic importance, Criccieth remained a small fishing port until the Victorians' craving for sun and sand saw it grow to today's proportions. There are two sand and shingle beaches either side of the castle and some excellent restaurants, cafés and bistros. Nearby Llanystumdwy was the boyhood home of former Prime Minister David Lloyd George.

Pwllheli has plenty of facilities, including an international-size marina. Although the town is good for shopping, it has a rather charmless urban sprawl, and there are better beaches elsewhere.

Abersoch is a lively resort whose fine sandy beach and dunes are

sheltered from the wild Atlantic winds by the Cilan headland, the eastern jaw of Hell's Mouth. The shelter has helped Abersoch grow into an international centre for yachting: there is some sort of regatta or race almost every summer weekend. The village itself is ringed around a large harbour. Abersoch also caters for a wide range of popular watersports.

49

TOURIST INFORMATION CENTRES

Caernarfon
Oriel Pendeitsh, Castle Street.
Tel: 01286 672232

Holyhead
Stena Line, Terminal 1, Holyhead, Isle of Anglesey. Tel: 01407 762622

Porthmadog
High Street. Tel: 01766 512981

Pwllheli
Station Square. Tel: 01758 613000

PLACES OF INTEREST

Beaumaris Castle
Castle Street.
Tel: 01248 810921;
www.beaumaris.com

Beaumaris Gaol and Courthouse
Steeple Lane. Tel: 01248 810361

Caernarfon Airworld Aviation Museum
Caernarfon Airport, Dinas Dinlle.
Tel: 01286 830800; www.air-world.co.uk

Caernarfon Castle
Tel: 01286 677617;
www.caernarfon.com

Criccieth Castle
Tel: 01766 522227

Din Llugwy Ancient Village
Nr Moelfre.

Lloyd George Museum and Highgate
Llanystumdwy nr Criccieth
Tel: 01766 522071

Plas Newydd
Llanfairpwll.
Tel: 01248 714795

Portmeirion
Tel: 01766 770000;
www.portmeirion-village.com

Seawatch
Moelfre.Tel: 01248 410277

Segontium Museum
Beddgelert Rd, Caernarfon
Tel: 01286 678416

FOR CHILDREN

Anglesey Model Village and Gardens
Newborough, Isle of Anglesey.
Tel: 01248 440477

Anglesey Sea Zoo
Brynsiencyn, Menai Strait.
Tel: 01248 430411;
www.angleseyseazoo.co.uk

Bodorgan, Isle of Anglesey
Tel: 01407 840440;
www.parc-henblas-park.co.uk
Pili Palas Butterfly and Minibeasts Centre
Menai Bridge, Isle of Anglesey.
Tel: 01248 712474

SHOPPING
Market Days
Caernarfon, Sat, also Mon in summer.
Pwllheli, Wed.
Pothmadog, Fri.
Holyhead, Mon.
Llangefni, Thu & Sat.

PERFORMING ARTS
Galeri
Doc Victoria, Caernarfon.
Tel: 01286 685252;
www.galericaernarfon.com

SPORTS & ACTIVITIES
ANGLING
Sea Fishing
Boat trips for anglers operate from
Amlwch, Beaumaris Cemaes and
Pwllheli.

Shore Fishing
Catches include bass, coalfish, cod,
conger eel, mackerel, mullet and
plaice.
Game Fishing
Anglesey has many lakes and inland
rivers. Llyn Alaw. Tel: 01407 730762
Cefni Reservoir, Anglesey, is good for
brown and rainbow trout.
www.llyncefni.co.uk

BEACHES
Aberdaron
Excellent sand and pebble beach,
popular with both bathers and surfers.
Abersoch
Sand dunes line a long sandy beach
that is shared with dinghy sailors. A
motor boat exclusion zone for bathers.
Excellent water quality.
Benllech
A blue flag beach with fine sands ideal
for families. A choice of food and ice
cream is available right by the beach.
Black Rock Sands, Morfa Bychan
Long, firm sandy beach that is ideal for
bathing, boating, beach-cast fishing
and watersports.

51

Borth y Guest, Porthmadog
Beautiful sandy bay.

Criccieth
Two pebble and sand beaches.

Dinas Dinlle, nr Caernarfon
Good sandy beach popular for watersports.

Llanbedrog
National Trust owned. Long sandy beach east of Pwllheli – sheltered and beautiful.

Moelfre/Lligwy
Small beach by the harbour. Coast path leads north to the sands of Traeth Lligwy.

Nefyn
A sweeping bay with 2 miles (3km) of sand. Excellent for watersports and bathing.

Porth Dinllaen
One of the most scenic sandy beaches in Wales with a pub right on the beach.

Porth Iago
Idyllic sunbathing but very small cliff-ringed sandy cove 4 miles (6.4km) north of Aberdaron.

Porth Neigwl (Hell's Mouth)
Wild Atlantic winds and waves make this ideal for surfing. Bathing is dangerous here with strong undertows and cross-currents.

Pwllheli
The South Beach mainly shingle; Glan-y-mor is muddy near the marina, sand improves towards Pen-y-chain headland.

Red Wharf Bay
A sand, mud and cobble beach ideal for walks. Pub and café/restaurant.

Rhosneigr
Exposed beach excellent for watersports like windsurfing.

Trearddur Bay
Big sands and seas ideal for canoeing and surfboarding.

Whistling Sands (Porth Oer)
Splendid, isolated beach. Café in high season. National Trust (pay car park).

BOAT TRIPS

Aberdaron to Bardsey Island.
Tel: 08458 1136554 or 07814 128620
Shearwater Coastal Cruises
Pwllheli Marina and Porthmadog.
Tel: 01758 740899

CYCLING
Traffic-free routes
Llon Las Menai
Caernarfon to Y Felinheli 4.5 miles
(7.6km) each way.
Tel: 01286 672255
Llon Las Cefni
A 12-mile (19km) ride across Anglesey
from Newborough to Llyn Cefni
(Information and leaflet from Sustrans)
Tel: 0117 929 0888;
www.sustrans.org.uk
Llon Eifion
A railway path from Caernarfon to
Bryncir 12 miles (19km) each way.
Tel: 01286 672255
HORSE-RIDING
Afonwen Riding Centre
Pwllheli. Tel: 01766 810939
Cilan Riding Centre
Abersoch. Tel: 01758 713276
Dwyfor Ranch
Llanystumdwy, Criccieth.
Tel: 01766 523349
Llanbedrog Riding Centre
Nr. Pwllheli.
Tel: 01758 740267

Tal-y-Foel Riding Centre
Dwyran, Anglesey.
Tel: 01248 430377
WALKING
Long Distance Routes
Lleyn Coastal Path,
Anglesey Coast Path.
WATERSPORTS
Sailing Centres
Abersoch, Pwllheli, Holyhead, Red
Wharf Bay, Beaumaris, Trearddur.

ANNUAL EVENTS & CUSTOMS
Abersoch Jazz Festival
Jazz on the beach, Jun.
www.abersochjazzfestival.com
Amlwch Viking Festival
Re-enacts the Battle of Ynys Mon of
AD 972, end of Jun.
Criccieth Festival
Music and arts festival, Jun.
Eisteddfod Mon
Music, dance and arts – held in a
different Anglesey town each year, May.
Holyhead Maritime Festival
Music and dance on Newry Beach,
last weekend, Jul.

Anne's Pantry
The Beach, Moelfre,
Anglesey, LL72 8HL
Tel: 01248 410386
Enjoy a hearty Welsh breakfast, jacket potatoes or sandwiches for lunch and an evening meal, in this relaxed cottage set back from the harbour. Summer visitors can enjoy dining in the garden. Sunday lunch is served in winter.

Caffi Cwrt Tearoom
Y Maes, Criccieth LL52 0AG
Tea, sandwiches and home-made cakes in a charming 18th-century cottage that used to be a Court of Petty Sessions. Just off the village green, the charming cottage has beamed ceilings and the tea garden has a grand view of Criccieth Castle.

Old Boat House
Red Wharf Bay, Pentraeth,
Gwynedd, LL75 8RJ
Tel: 01248 852731
Set back from the wide sweep of Red Wharf Bay, you couldn't ask for a better view. Sandwiches and snacks are available or more substantial meals, including cannelloni, curries, lasagne and lemon chicken. Sit in the garden on fine summer days or in a cosy bistro-like restaurant.

Sea View Tearooms
Borth y Guest, LL49 9TR
Tel: 012144 51332
Promenade café serving sandwiches, cakes and simple hot meals, such as liver and bacon. Stunning views from the terrace across the bay to the Snowdonian mountains.

Y Gegin Fawr
Aberdaron, LL53 8BE
Tel: 01758 760359
This 14th-century building once catered for Bardsey pilgrims. Simply decorated on two floors, specialities include locally caught crab and lobster, home-made cakes and scones.

Black Boy
**Northgate St, Caernarfon,
Gwynedd, LL55 1RW
Tel: 01286 673604**
This lively 16th-century inn, with
beamed ceilings and stone fireplaces,
serves Bass beers and a wide range of
traditional bar meals, and more exotic
favourites, such as a Thai green curry.

The Ship Inn
**Red Wharf Bay, Anglesey, LL75 8RJ
Tel: 01248 852568**
Superbly located on the shore of Red
Wharf Bay, this whitewashed inn
has dark, oak beams, wooden floors
and cottage-style furniture. From
outside tables you can munch on
gourmet sandwiches and baguettes
while looking out across the bay.
The restaurant and bar menus are
renowned for their locally caught fish.

Trearddur Bay Hotel
**Lon Isallt, Anglesey,
LL65 2UN
Tel: 01407 860301
www.trearddurbayhotel.co.uk**
This large hotel dominates the shore of
Trearddur Bay. Within the complex, the
lively Inn at the Bay offers bar meals
in an informal setting, while the Snug
is ideal for those wanting a traditional
pub atmosphere. The restaurant menu
features locally caught seafood and
Welsh beef and lamb.

Ty Coch
**Porthdinllaen, Morfa Nefyn, Pwllheli,
Gwynedd, LL53 6DB
Tel: 01758 720498**
One of Wales' famous pubs, with great
atmosphere and a truly wonderful
beachfront position. Light meals
include ploughman's, and mussels in
garlic butter served with green salad.
Tea and coffee are available. The pub
was featured in the Demi Moore film
Half Light.

Snowdonia:
Mountains & Valleys

INTRODUCTION

Snowdonia has a hard heart of rock that has enticed generations of walkers and climbers on to its spectacular arêtes and crags, and has provided slate for local building. Here is the land where the warrior princes of Gwynedd scored great victories in battles against the Norman kings, who were forced to build the formidable 'iron ring' of coastal castles from Harlech to Conwy.

Unmissable attractions

This area has been the inspiration to poets, artists and travellers...visit the marvellous town Conwy and explore historic Conwy Castle...marvel at Swallow Falls at Betws-y-Coed...climb Cadair Idris, the most romantic of the Welsh peaks...explore Harlech Castle, which stands overlooking the historic town...travel on the Snowdon Mountain Railway or climb to Snowdon's summit...walk around Bala lake, the largest natural lake in Wales...cycle around the beautiful countryside that lies around Beddglert...take a miner's tramway deep into the award-winning Slate Caverns at Blaenau Ffestiniog.

1

1 Llynnau Mymbyr

The twin lakes of Llynnau Mymbyr, at the foot of Snowdon, are only separated in very dry summers. The lake is also popular with canoeists.

2 Conwy

With its two barbicans, eight massive towers and great bow-shaped hall, a visit to the historic Conwy Castle and town should not be missed.

3 Beddgelert
The beautiful countryside that lies around Beddgelert in the Snowdonia National Park, offers plenty of great routes for cyclists.

4 Llanberis
The still waters of Llyn Padarn, can be seen from the A4086, but it is best explored on foot on the trail around this beautiful lake.

5

6

5 Llanrwst

This attractive arched bridge, built in 1636 probably to a design by Inigo Jones, spans the River Conwy by the busy market town of Llanrwst.

6 Betws-y-Coed

Mingle with walkers and climbers at Betws-y-Coed, the most popular of Snowdonia's resorts, and don't miss the spectacular Swallow Falls.

ABERDYFI

In the most southwestern corner of the Snowdonia National Park, Aberdyfi is the finest of Merionydd's coastal resorts. The picturesque, pastel colour-washed cottages, shops and inns, and small harbour are tucked beneath the steep grassy slopes of the Tarren Hills and the sands of the Dyfi Estuary and Cardigan Bay. Those beaches extend northwards for almost 4 miles (6km) to Tywyn. Besides swimming, sunbathing and sandcastle building, Aberdyfi is popular for most watersports, including sailing, sail-boarding, canoeing and fishing. On most weekends yachts with a multitude of colourful sails can be seen gliding across the waves.

Inland from Aberdyfi, the Happy Valley delves into the Tarren Hills. Its river, the Afon Dyffryn-gwyn, flows from Llyn Barfog, which means the Bearded lake. Some say that the name Barfog could relate to Barfog, the colleague of King Arthur. Ancient tales abound about Arthur slaying the mythical beast, Afanc, on this spot and there's even a nearby summit rock named Carn March Arthur, the cairn of Arthur's horse. Could it be more simple, and that the long rushes that infest the lake's edge form the beard?

On the other side of the Happy Valley lane the Tarrens proper begin. These superb, grassy whalebacks span some 10 miles (16km) to the Dysynni Valley and offer some of the best wilderness ridge-walking in this part of Wales. Although blighted by conifer forests in places, there are many Neolithic cairns and stunning views of mountain coast and estuary, especially at sunset.

BALA

Bala's jewel is its lake, Llyn Tegid, the largest natural lake in Wales. This beautiful lake, surrounded by the Aran and Arenig Mountains, is popular for watersports, especially when strong southwesterly winds whip up the waves into white horses. The lake is popular with anglers too. Pike, perch, trout, salmon and roach are plentiful, but Llyn Tegid is most famous for the Gwyniad, which resembles a freshwater herring and is believed to have been trapped here since the last Ice Age.

The village is dominated by the wide main street, whose austere architecture is camouflaged by the brightly coloured signs of cafés, gift shops and inns. Bala has religious roots, a fact reinforced by the number of chapels and the statue of Dr Lewis Edwards, founder of the Methodist College, and, opposite the White Lion, a statue of the Reverend Thomas Charles, one the founders of the British and Foreign Bible Society.

The Bala Lake Railway is one of the narrow-gauge steam railways for which the Welsh are famous. It has its terminus on the south shore of the lake just over a half-mile (800m) from the village. Trains run for 4.5 miles (7km) along the southern shore to Llanuwychllyn on the trackbed of the former Ruabon–Barmouth line. The service operates between April and September. Close to Bala Station, the motte-and-bailey castle of Tomen y Mur has a long history – some historians believe that the mound dates from Roman times. The castle was one of the several captured from the Normans by Llewelyn ap Iowerth (Llewelyn the Great) in 1202.

Visit

TALYLLYN RAILWAY

The narrow-gauge Talyllyn Railway opened in 1865 to carry slate from the Bryn Eglwys quarries near Abergynolwyn to the sea at Tywyn, a journey of around 7 miles (11km). The railway and the quarries closed in 1946 following a serious rock fall, but a few years later a group of enthusiasts formed the Talyllyn Railway Preservation Society (the first such organisation in the world) and took over the running of the steam railway, which still carries thousands of wide-eyed passengers through the beautiful Fathew Valley, stopping at Dolgoch Falls.

BARMOUTH

The Snowdonia National Park borders bypass Barmouth on the side of the Rhinog Mountain. The largely Victorian resort built into the rocks is a bit too much like Blackpool? When walking along the promenade past the funfair and the fish-and-chip cafés, visitors could be forgiven for thinking they were on the Fylde Coast, and Barmouth has been blessed with the same wonderful sands. Those who look for more than a beach holiday and who choose to explore a little further, will find true majesty in the surrounding mountains and the Mawddach Estuary. The Rhinogydd range, which rises from the backyards of the resort, features some of the finest.

A web of stairs and alleyways leads from the High Street up to Hen Bermo, the old town, built almost vertically and haphazardly up the cliffs. Eventually you will come to Dinas Oleu (the Fortress of light), donated to the National Trust by the local Talbot family.

Insight

THE ARAN MOUNTAINS

Towering above Bala's lake, Aran Fawddwy at 2,969 feet (905m) is Wales' highest mountain south of Snowdon. The River Dee has its birthplace in a small lake that cowers beneath the summit crags. Once locals mistakenly believed that nearby Cadair Idris was a few feet higher, and, jealous of its popularity, erected a huge cairn to redress the balance. The rocky Aran ridge includes another fine conical-shaped mountain, Aran Benllyn, which is the one that dominates Bala's lake view.

As there wasn't enough room to squeeze the main road from Harlech between the foothills and the sea, all roads climbed inland, over the Rhinog mountain passes. However, in the mid-19th century a coast road was built borrowing ground from the beach area.

In 1867 the railways followed, crossing over the Mawddach Estuary on a half-mile (800m) new bridge

69

which had a swing section to allow shipping to pass. The new breed of Victorian tourist flocked here for the sea air, the beaches and the bathing. Hotels were shoehorned into the narrow strait, built almost into the rock-face. One of those visitors was William Wordsworth, who described the view across the estuary towards Cadair Idris as sublime and equal to any in Scotland.

Artists J M W Turner and Richard Wilson came to capture the changing light and renowned beauty of both estuary and mountainside.

BEDDGELERT

Beddgelert has a location to die for, tucked away near the confluence of the Glaslyn and Colwyn valleys, and beneath the lusciously wooded lower crags and bluffs of Snowdon. The centrepiece of the village is a twin-arched stone bridge over the lively Glaslyn. Huddled around the bridge are the stone-built cottages, inns, craft shops and cafés. Beddgelert and the area around it once made it

to Hollywood, for many scenes from Ingrid Bergman's film, *The Inn of the Sixth Happiness,* were shot here.

Beddgelert, which means Gelert's grave, takes its name from the Celtic saint, Kelert. Some would have you believe that Gelert was Llewelyn the Great's faithful dog, killed by his master, who mistakenly believed it had butchered his child. The myth and the building of the grave were ploys by David Pritchard, the first landlord of the Royal Goat Hotel, built in 1803, to bring more visitors to his new establishment.

The Sygun Copper Mines to the north of Beddgelert are well worth seeing. You'll go on foot on a self-guided audio-visual tour through winding tunnels to see the veins of copper ore in chambers that are coloured by a fascinating array of stalactites and stalagmites.

Looking downwards onto the copper mine from Snowdon's slopes is Dinas Emrys, a rocky wooded knoll capped with the ruins of an old fort, possibly from the Iron Age and probably used in the time of Llewelyn the Great. Legends tell that it was the refuge of Arthurian magician Merlin, and of Vortigern, a 5th-century British king who was fleeing from the Danes. Access to the area is difficult, sometimes even dangerous, and is not advised.

To the south of the village the A498 Porthmadog road enters the Aberglaslyn Pass, where the flanks of Moel Hebog and the 700-foot (213m) splintered cliffs form a cavernous rocky gorge, through which the waters of the River Glaslyn transform into violent white torrents. In the next few years the Welsh Highland Railway will recommence its journey through the pass.

BETWS-Y-COED

Betws-y-Coed, pronounced 'betoose ee koyd', is the most popular of all the Snowdonian resorts and on most days its main street, the A5, will be choc-a-bloc with traffic. Sheltered by enormous hillside forests and sited near to the confluences of the

Conwy and two of its tributaries, the Lledr and the Llugwy, Betws-y-Coed is renowned for its waterfalls. One flows beneath the Pont-y-Pair (the bridge of the cauldron), which was built in 1468 at the village centre. This is popular with sunbathers who lounge on the crags that line the banks. The Swallow Falls, best viewed from the north bank of the Llugwy, is a spectacular torrent, lying 2 miles (3km) west up the road, while the Conwy Falls are on the Penmachno end of the village, accessed from the car park of the Otter Restaurant and Café.

Each day walkers and climbers congregate before and after their mountain adventures. There are more gear shops than food stores. Nightlife tends to centre on the Royal Oak's Stables Bar – those wanting a seat will have to get there early.

One of the popular attractions is the motor museum. Created from the private collection of the Houghton family, it includes several exotic and rare cars.

BETWS-Y-COED

Lead played a big part in Betws-y-Coed's early development and if you take one of the forest walks up to Llyn Parc you'll see many of the relics from the old mines. Further east is Llyn Crafnant, a beautiful mountain lake reached by narrow winding lanes from Betws or on foot along a bridleway from the next village west, Capel Curig.

Capel Curig is the true gateway to the big mountains of Snowdonia and as such is considered to be the best-placed resort for weekend mountain walkers and climbers who want an early start.

BLAENAU FFESTINIOG

Arrive at Blaenau Ffestiniog on a rainy day and you'll see nothing but slate. The houses are built from it, they're roofed with it and their gardens and backyards are piled up with it – great slag heaps that disappear into the low slate-grey clouds. Slate is Blaenau's heritage and they're proud of it. The slate has been mined and quarried from the

Moelwyn and Manod mountains that lie either side of the 900 foot-high (275m) valley head where the town stands. When the cloud lifts, the mountains reveal themselves to be finely sculpted with distinctive shapes – suddenly Blaenau's situation looks considerably more appealing to walkers and climbers.

This slate town has its ghostly relics. Take a look at the valley of Cwmorthin, just beyond the suburb of Tanygrisiau. A slatey track climbs beneath the Moelwyn crags past a forlorn-looking lake into a valley devastated by quarries and mines. Beyond the high-chimneyed shell of the old barracks, you can also see the rusting pulley wheels and the bogies of the old slate carts.

Blaenau lies at the end of the narrow-gauge Ffestiniog Railway from Porthmadog, a splendid journey around the Moelwyn and through the beautiful oak woods and pastures of the Ffestiniog Valley. The journey takes you past Tanygrisiau's lake and power station. These form

Visit

UNDERGROUND TOURS

At the award-winning Llechwedd Slate Caverns at Blaenau Ffestiniog, visitors take a miners' tramway deep into the slate mountain, where a miner guides them around 19th-century caverns of cathedral-like proportions. There's also a Deep Mine tour starting with Britain's steepest railway (1:1.8). A 25-minute underground walk reveals the social condition in which the miners lived as told by 'the ghost of a Victorian miner'. Re-created Victorian shops plus a licensed restaurant and a pub complete the experience.

part of a hydroelectric scheme where cheap-rate power is used to pump water up to the higher tarn, Llyn Stwlan, whose head of water is then stored until needed.

Blaenau's smaller neighbour, Llan Ffestiniog, is a typical Welsh village with a small square and a large chapel, surrounded by verdant scenery. Roaring deep in the valley,

below the church, are the waterfalls known as Rhaeadr Cynfal, plunging into a 200-foot (60m) ravine. The large rock pillar at the top of the falls, Huw Llwyd's Pulpit, was named after a 17th-century warrior and poet who lived in the village.

CONWY

Few rivers can match the Conwy. Its source, Llyn Conwy, lies high in moorland known as the Migneint but soon it is tumbling down the wooded mountainsides to Betws-y-Coed. Here it calms, passing through lush pastures before lazily meandering across sandbars and mudflats out into the estuary between Conwy and the headland of Great Orme.

Conwy, the town, is one of the great treasures of Wales; a place where history parades itself around every corner. Three fine bridges, including Thomas Telford's magnificent suspension bridge of 1822 and Stephenson's tubular railway bridge, cross the estuary beneath the castle, allowing both

BLAENAU FFESTINIOG

CONWY CASTLE

Visit

CAER LLEION FORT

Conwy Mountain forms the backdrop to the town and its castle. High on the hillside are the remains of a much older civilisation, for here lies Caer Lleion fort. Evidence shows that boundary walls surround more than 50 Iron Age hut circles. The walls have almost, but not quite, crumbled into the hillside from which they came. The wooden huts, with their roofs thatched with rushes and reeds, have not survived.

road and the railway into this medieval World Heritage Site.

Conwy's castle has the shape we expect in our fairy-tale castles. It dates back to 1287 when powerful English king, Edward I, built it as part of his 'iron ring' to repress the rebellious troops of Llewelyn the Great, who had given him a great deal of trouble in his conquest of Wales. A statue of the revered Welsh prince dominates Lancaster Square.

Great town walls 6-feet (2m) thick and 35-feet (10.7m) high with three original gates and numerous towers still encircle the old town. The walkway along the top of the walls offers splendid over-the-rooftops views of the castle, the Conwy Estuary and the rocky knolls of Deganwy. At the wall's end, steps descend to the quayside where fishermen sort their nets and squawking seagulls watch out for the scraps. In summer there is a good selection of boat trips, some just around the estuary; others further afield to Anglesey.

Conwy has many old buildings. The half-timbered Aberconwy House (National Trust) has origins in the 14th century, although most of its structure belongs to around 1500. The equally impressive Plas Mawr is a large mansion, built for the Wynne family in 1576. Now in the hands of CADW, the building has very fine interior plasterwork.

St Mary's Church occupies a central but quiet position in the town, on the site of a Cistercian Abbey of which it was once a part; the abbey was moved by Edward I to accommodate his castle.

DINAS MAWDDWY

Dinas Mawddwy, a small village just off the main highway (A470) lies sheltered from the westerly winds by the high pass, Bwlch Oerddrws, in a sylvan hollow close to the valleys of the Cerist and the Dyfi rivers. It's a centre for walkers and climbers who flock to Cwm Cywarch where giant crags soar to the Aran ridges.

The Dyfi valley is simply delectable in these parts. The sleek profiled velvety hills with a patchwork of heather, bracken and moor grass, are mellowed by hedgerow, oak woods and whitewashed farm cottages – this is truly God's country. Indeed it used to be the stamping ground of St Tydecho, cousin of St Cadfan and one of three saints sent from Brittany in the 6th century to introduce Christianity to Wales. The ancient stone church in Llanymawddwy, a few miles upstream, is dedicated to the saint.

DOLGELLAU

Dolgellau sits snugly among pastureland that rises from the banks of the Mawddach and Wnion to the great cliffs of Cadair Idris. An impressive seven-arched bridge, Y Bont Fawr, built in 1638 but heavily modified in subsequent centuries, crosses the Wnion and leads into the market town. Narrow austere streets of stone and slate buildings lead into a large central square.

Dolgellau's origins as a village lie in the 12th century when it was attached to the Cistercian monastery at Cymer Abbey. Very little remains in the town from that period – even the old Parliament building, Cwrt Plas yn Dre, where Owain Glyn Dwr plotted the downfall of the English in 1398, was pulled down in 1881. The town grew during the 18th and 19th centuries from the proceeds of a large wool industry – celebrated

CADAIR IDRIS

every year in the local 'Wool Race' – and a gold rush of the same era. At its peak more than 500 men were employed in the gold and copper mines in the hills around Dolgellau.

The town had a significant Quaker community at one time. A museum in Eldon Square tells how they were persecuted. Rowland Ellis, one of their number, emigrated to Pennsylvania in 1686, where he founded the famous Bryn Mawr women's college at the University of Pennsylvania.

Come to Dolgellau early on a Sunday morning and you'll see scores of walkers, stocking up with bread, cakes and soft drinks in readiness for a trip up Cadair Idris. Steeped in Celtic legends and myths, Cadair Idris, The Seat of Idris, is the most romantic of Welsh peaks. Though not quite reaching the heights of central Snowdonia, Cadair has all the grandeur of Snowdon and a little bit more – fine crag-bound tarns, sheer rock faces and wide-sweeping views across

what seems like the whole of Wales – it's set in a green, fertile landscape of oak woods, dashing streams and pretty stone cottages dotted across pastoral foothills. The main starting points for Cadair are Minffordd, which lies just north of Tal-y-llyn, and Pont Dyffrydan car park on the Old Cader Road, the start of the route known as the Pony Path.

HARLECH

Harlech Castle stands on a 200-foot (61m) crag defiantly watching out over Tremadog Bay. It's one of the most dramatic castles in the Britain. Although the outer walls are badly damaged, the majestic inner curtain wall and their great round corner towers are well preserved. Built for Edward I around 1280, the castle would have been protected by what were then sea cliffs (the sea has since receded to reveal coastal plain and sand dunes), while a deep moat protected the rear landward side. The castle kept the Welsh at bay until 1404 when it was taken by

83

Visit

MORFA HARLECH

This area of sand dunes, salt marshes and mudflats reaches out into Tremadog Bay. The dune system is rich in flora, including the purple-pink flowers of the pyramidal and green-winged orchids. The mudflats in the north are good for wading birds and wildfowl. Polecats have been spotted here, as have many species of butterfly, including the dark-green fritillary. As it's part of a National Nature Reserve, permits are required to stray off the beach and away from the rights of way.

the holiday quarter, including a hotel, campsites, apartments and the railway, spreads across the plains. Visitors come here for the magnificent beaches whose position, with the mountains of Snowdonia spanning the skyline across Tremadog Bay, is quite spectacular.

Behind the village, narrow country lanes wind through the impressive Rhinog Mountains, a range that consists of thick beds of gritstone and shale formed in the Cambrian era – some of the world's oldest surface rocks. The gnarled and faulted crags are riven by deep transverse canyons that create repeated obstacles to those wanting to walk along the 'ridge'. Boulders and scree from the eroded gritstone slabs are frequently covered with knee-deep heather. Early roads, paths and tracks all ran east–west, following the natural lie of the land. The Roman Steps is one such route, climbing out of the valley of Cwm Bychan and crossing the range at the wild pass, Bwlch Tyddiad. This

the Welsh leader Owain Glyn Dwr, who then had himself crowned here as Prince of Wales, witnessed by noblemen from Scotland, France and Spain. A long siege here during the Wars of the Roses inspired the famous Welsh marching song *Men of Harlech*.

The village of Harlech village is quite small. The old quarter lies on the hillside by the castle, while

ROMAN STEPS

packhorse route (no it's not Roman) was constructed in medieval times and offers a splendid route into the mountains in fine, dry weather for experienced walkers.

LLANBERIS & SNOWDON

The successes and failures of Llanberis have always been linked to its mountains. From the moment in the late 18th century that they decided to quarry the slate from Elidir Fawr, Llanberis was transformed from a tiny village to the bustling lakeside town it is today. In its prime the Dinorwig Quarry employed 3,000 men, many of whom travelled from as far afield as Anglesey. When the slate quarry finally closed without warning in August 1969, mountain tourism was ready to take its place.

In Victorian times, popular interest in mountains was in its infancy. Being Wales' highest peak, the tourists' attention was drawn to Snowdon and Llanberis, the village at its foot. When 19th-century traveller, George Borrow, came here he observed that people were going up or descending the mountain as far as the eye could see.

The Snowdon Mountain Railway, Britain's only rack-and-pinion railway, opened in 1896. Unfortunately, the first day proved disastrous, for an out-of-control descending train derailed itself before tumbling down the steep slopes. One passenger who jumped from a falling carriage was tragically killed. Today many thousands of passengers listen to the running commentary as their steam engine travels through woodland and over a viaduct before puffing up the mountain. A new summit hotel with wide, picture windows has recently replaced the old 'hovel'.

The slate industry lives on through the town's Welsh Slate Museum, which occupies the same Dinorwig site on the northeast shore of Llyn Padarn. Here you can get an insight into the miner's life and his work, watch a craftsman split

SNOWDON

MOUNTAIN RAILWAY

LLANBERIS

· To the Summit since 1896 ·

the rock into fine tiles and see the largest waterwheel on mainland Britain. The museum stands on the edge of the Padarn Country Park, where footpaths climb through woodland to reveal splendid views across Llanberis twin glacial lakes towards Snowdon.

And there's another narrow-gauge steam train to ride, the Llanberis Lake Railway chugs along the shores of Llyn Padarn, from the town centre to Penllyn at the lake's northwestern tip.

LLANRWST

Llanrwst has always flirted with tourism but has never stepped out of the shadow of neighbour Betws-y-Coed. It is claimed that the three-arched bridge over the Conwy was designed by Inigo Jones, and although there's little evidence of this, it certainly is elegant. The 15th-century ivy and Virginia creeper-clad cottage of Ty Hwnt i'r Bont next to the bridge is very pretty and a National Trust tea house.

Set back from the western banks of the Conwy, Gwydir Castle was for centuries the grand seat of the Wynn family. It dates to Tudor times, but much of the house was rebuilt in the 19th century. The important 1640s panelled dining room has been reinstalled in the castle, following its repatriation from the New York Metropolitan Museum.

A few miles north down the Conwy Valley at Caerhun, is the site of a Roman fort, *Canovium*, established soon after the invasion of Wales under Cnaeus Julius Agricola between AD 75 and 77. The Roman cohorts marched into the hills, tamed the Ordovices tribesmen who farmed the high Carneddau slopes, and built a surfaced road over Bwlch y Ddeufaen, which would link with their fort at Segontium (Caernarfon). Today the platform by the banks of the Conwy is still evident, but obscured in one corner by the building of an 11th-century Church of Saint Mary within its confines.

TOURIST INFORMATION CENTRES

Bala
Pensarn Road.
Tel: 01678 521021

Betws-y-Coed
Royal Oak Stables.
Tel: 01690 710426

Conwy
Conwy Castle.
Tel: 01492 592248

Dolgellau
Eldon Square,
Tel: 01341 422888

Llanberis
1b High Street.
Tel: 01286 870765

PLACES OF INTEREST

Aberconwy House
Castle Street, Conwy.
Tel: 01492 592246
Fourteenth-century merchant's house
– one of the finest examples in Wales.

Conwy Castle
Castle Street, Conwy.
Tel: 01492 592246

Conwy Valley Railway Museum
Betws-y-Coed Station Yard.
Tel: 01690 710568

Electric Mountain
Llanberis.
Tel: 01286 870636;
www.wales-underground.org.uk/
electric/information.shtml.
Guided tours around an underground
hydro-electric power station.

Llechwedd Slate Caverns
Blaenau Ffestiniog.
Tel: 01766 830306;
www.llechwedd-slate-caverns.co.uk
A tour of the underground world of the
slate miner.

Motor Museum
Betws-y-Coed.
Tel: 01690 710760
Exhibits include Bugatti, Aston Martin,
Bentley, Bullnose Morris, Ford T and
British motorbikes.

Plas Mawr
High Street, Conwy.
Tel: 01492 580167
This is possibly the best-preserved
Elizabethan townhouse in Britain.

Quaker Heritage Centre
Sgwar Elson, Dolgellau.
Tel: 01341 424442
Tells the story of the local Quaker community that lived here, of their persecution and finally, their emigration to Pennsylvannia.

Snowdon Mountain Railway
Llanberis.
Tel: 0870 4580033;
www.snowdonrailway.co.uk

Trefriw Woollen Mills
Trefriw.
Tel: 01492 640462;
www.t-w-m.co.uk
The mill specialises in the manufacture of Welsh double weave (tapestry) bedspreads (carthenni) and tweeds. Visitors can tour the mill and see goods being made or buy from the shop.

Welsh Slate Museum
Dinorwig Quarry, Llanberis.
Tel: 01286 870630
The museum gives an insight into a miner's life.

SHOPPING
Market Days
Bangor, Sun Farmers' Market.
Blaenau Ffestiniog, Tue.
Barmouth, Thu and Sun in summer.
Conwy, Tue.
Llanrwst, Tue.

LOCAL SPECIALITIES
Trefriw Woollen Mill (see above) and Meirion Mill at Dinas Mawddwy have a tempting array of lovely Welsh fabrics and tapestries.

PERFORMING ARTS
The Dragon Theatre
Jubilee Rd, Barmouth.
Tel: 01341 281697

Theatre Ardudwy
Harlech.
Tel: 01766 780667;
www.theatrardudwy.co.uk

SPORTS & ACTIVITIES
ANGLING
Bala Lake
The lake stocks large pike, also perch, eel and grayling.

Crafnant Fishery
Llyn Crafnant, above Conwy Valley near Trefriw.
Tel: 01492 640818. Lake with brown and rainbow trout.

BEACHES
Aberdyfi
An extensive sandy beach, ideal for families.

Barmouth
Long sandy beach away from the estuary.

Conwy
Good beach with sand dunes 1 mile (1.6km) west of the town, beyond the marina.

Fairbourne
Good sandy beach, ideal for swimming.

Harlech
A straight beach with miles of golden sand, ideal for swimming.

Tywyn
Cobbles with good sand at low tide, popular beach for families.

CYCLING
Excellent for mountain biking. There are many routes in Coed y Brenin (forest) where there's a visitor centre, café and bike shop. Tel: 01341 440728; www.beicsbrenin.co.uk

GOLF
Ffestiniog Golf Club
Y Cefn, Festiniog.
Tel: 01766 762637
9 holes.

Tyddyn Mawr Golf Club
Crawia Road, Llanrug, Caernarfon.
Tel: 01286 674919
9 holes.

HORSE-RIDING
E Prichard Pony Trekking
Felen Rhyd Fach,
Maentwrog.
Tel: 01766 590231

The Trekking Centre
Abergwynant Farm, Penmaenpool, Dolgellau.
Tel: 01341 422377

Ty Coch Farm
Penmachno,
Nr Betws-y-Coed.
Tel: 01690 760248

WALKING

The area is the best in Wales for mountain walking. Snowdon, the Glyderau and the Carneddau ranges are the most popular. Never under-estimate the dangers of walking and climbing in the mountains.

WATERSPORTS

SAILING CENTRES

Aberdyfi
Harbourmaster.
Tel: 01654 767626

Barmouth
Harbourmaster.
Tel: 01341 280671

Conwy
Harbourmaster.
Tel: 01492 596253

WHITE WATER RAFTING

Canolfan Tryweryn
Frongoch, Bala.
Tel: 01678 521083;
www.ukrafting.co.uk

ANNUAL FESTIVALS & EVENTS

Conwy
River Festival, early Aug.
Tel: 01492 596253;
www.conwyriverfestival.org

Llanberis
Film Festival, early Mar, various venues.
Tel: 01286 685503;
www.llamff.co.uk

Dolgellau
Sesiwn Fawr, Jul. Folk and rock festival held around Eldon Square.
Tel: 08712 301314;
www.sesiwnfawr.co.uk

Cemlyn Restaurant and Tea Shop
High Street, Harlech,
LL46 2YA

An award-winning tea shop serving over 20 varieties of teas, along with coffees, delicious home-made cakes and sandwiches. Try local specialities such as bara brith or fruit cake, perhaps on a sun terrace with its spectacular views of Harlech Castle, Cardigan Bay and the grand Snowdonian mountains.

Lyn's Café and Teagarden
Liverpool House, Church Street,
Beddgelert, LL55 4YA
Tel: 01766 890374

Sited by the attractive River Colwyn in Beddgelert, the cosy café has a lovely riverside garden where you can relax with a coffee or tea. Alternatively, choose from a menu of breakfast items, snacks, light meals, clotted cream teas and evening meals. The café is licensed in the evening.

Pete's Eats
40 High Street,
Llanberis, LL55 4EU

This is one of the best chippys in the world, and, if you're in a mood to be self-indulgent, look no further. It's lively with good communal spirit among the climbers and hillwalkers who mix with the locals. There's an array of mountain snaps on the wall.

Pinnacle Café
Capel Curig, LL24 0EN
Tel: 01690 720201

This lively walkers' and climbers' café serves good café grub, including all-day breakfasts, piping-hot mugs of tea and hot chocolate fudge cake. Ideal for big pre-walk or after-walk appetites.

The Castle Hotel
High Street, Conwy, LL32 8DB
Tel: 01492 582800
www.castlewales.co.uk

A grand 16th-century coaching inn adorned with antiques and some fine paintings by Victorian artist John Dawson-Watson, who it is said painted to pay for his lodgings here. You can dine in Shakespeare's brasserie-type restaurant. Alternatively, there's a popular bar which serves excellent meals, but be early to grab a table.

The Groes Inn
Tyn y Groes, Conwy, LL32 8TN
Tel: 01492 650545
www.groesinn.com

Dating back to 1573, The Groes Inn, which overlooks Conwy Valley, became the first licensed inn in Wales. A traditional but luxurious inn, garlanded with flowerboxes in summer, it still retains the customary beamed ceilings and log fires. Anything from a light snack to gourmet meals (with many seafood specials) can be enjoyed in the bar or restaurant. Not ideal for kids.

Stables Bar, Royal Oak
Betws-y-Coed, LL24 0AY
Tel: 01690 710219

In an extension to Betws-y-Coed's largest hotel, the Stables Bar efficiently produces tasty bar meals time after time, even though the bar is usually extremely busy. On summer evenings there's a large outside dining area where you can eat under the trees and the stars.

White Horse Inn
Capel Garmon,
Betws-y-Coed, LL26 0RW
Tel: 01690 710271

A cosy 400-year-old inn in the village of Capel Garmon: one with beamed ceilings, log fires and a panoramic view of the Conwy Valley and the mountains of Snowdonia. The inn is well known for its fine food, with emphasis on good local produce. It also serves a wide selection of fine wines and real ales.

Northeast Wales
& Marches

CEIRIOG VALLEY

CHIRK

DENBIGH

KNIGHTON & OFFA'S DYKE

LLANDUDNO

LLANGOLLEN

WELSHPOOL

INTRODUCTION

In the fertile landscapes of old Clwyd and the Welsh Marches the sweet shires of England have gently melded into hill country; rolling hills that rise to the high ridges of the Berwyn Mountains and the Clwydians. Hillside fortresses highlight the times of border conflict: visits to the great houses and castles of Powis, Chirk, Denbigh and Ruthin are a must-sees for visitors.

HOT SPOTS

Unmissable attractions

If it's good old-fashioned fun you're after rather than culture, the north coast's golden beaches at Llandudno, Rhyl and Prestatyn await your arrival...visit the great manor houses and castles of Powis, Chirk, Denbigh and Ruthin...cycle along the top of the Dee Valley and enjoy the views of verdant hills...marvel at the waterfall at Pystyll Rhaeadr or the Pontcysyllte Aqueduct, Thomas Telford's feat of engineering over the deep Gorge of the River Dee...explore the Montgomeryshire hills on the Welshpool and Llanfair Light Railway...walk part – or all, if you have the time – of Offa's Dyke National Trail...discover Llanarmon Dyffryn Ceiriog, the most beautiful village in the valley...explore the elegant Victorian town of Llandudno.

1

1 Welshpool
The Welshpool and Llanfair Light Railway steams its way through picturesque countryside.

2 Llangollen
Thomas Telford built the Pontcysyllte Aqueduct, near Llangollen, in 1795. This inspired construction carries the great Llangollen Canal over the deep gorge of the River Dee.

3 Offa's Dyke
The Offa's Dyke National Trail winds its way through some spectacular Welsh landscapes.

4 Llandudno
The sweeping sands of Llandudno Bay are protected by the headlands of Great Orme and Little Orme.

5 Pistyll Rhaeadr
Situated in the Berwyn Mountains, Pistyll Rhaeadr, the highest waterfall in Wales, plunges through a gorge.

PISTYLL RHAEADR

CEIRIOG VALLEY

'A piece of heaven that has fallen to earth' is how the last British Liberal Prime Minister, Lloyd George, described the Ceiriog Valley. The Ceiriog river, which has its birthplace deep in the heart of the Berwyn Mountains, is a tributary of the Dee. Here it flows through a pastoral countryside, dotted with small farms, that wouldn't go amiss in a Constable landscape. It's not surprising that the valley has, over the centuries, inspired three local bards: Huw Morus (1662–1709), the Reverend Robert Ellis (1812–75) and John Ceiriog Hughes (1832–87).

Glyn Ceiriog is the largest village. It expanded in the 19th century with the mining of slate and other minerals in the area. There are still remnants of a tramway that was built to convey the slate to the main line at Chirk.

Llanarmon Dyffryn Ceiriog is the most beautiful village in the valley, with a church, two old-world pubs and several whitewashed cottages

Visit

ONE OF THE SEVEN WONDERS

George Borrow, author of *Wild Wales* (1862) saw the remote falls of Pistyll Rhaeadr and described the torrent as a 'immense skein of silk'. The waterfall lies 4 miles (6.5km) northwest of Llanrhaeadr-ym-Mochnant, is one of the Seven Wonders of Wales. Here the Afon Disgynfa tumbles 250 feet (76m) from the marshy wilderness of its glacial hanging valley, down tree-clad cliffs into the shadows of Tan y Pistyll, dwarfing the Welsh slate farmhouse at its foot. Most wonderfully, that farmhouse is also a licensed café.

clustering around a picture-postcard square. Lying by the confluence of the Ceiriog and a tributary, the Gwrachen, the village takes its name from the 5th-century missionary, St Garmon. A mound in the churchyard, known as Tomen Garmon, is a Bronze Age burial mound which is believed to be the place from where the missionary once stood to preach.

CHIRK

The border town of Chirk perches on a hillside separating the River Dee from the Ceiriog. It is a 'must' for canal enthusiasts who can marvel at Thomas Telford's ten-arched aqueduct, built in 1801 to convey the canal more than 70 feet (21m) above the valley bottom. Alongside there's an even taller viaduct, built by Henry Robertson in 1840 for the railway. Both were used to carry coal from the Flintshire coalfields.

Chirk Castle, which overlooks the town and the Ceiriog Valley, was built in 1310 by Edward I's Justice of Wales, Roger Mortimer, to replace an 11th-century wooden motte-and-bailey castle south of the town. The walls have since been decorated by scores of glazed mullioned windows, hiding the stark face those powerful circular towers would have issued. The castle has been continuously inhabited since 1595 by the Myddleton family, whose heraldic icon, 'the bloody red hand' can be seen on many pub signs.

DENBIGH

Denbighshire's medieval county town basks in the heart of the Vale of Clwyd, a wide and verdant valley dividing the rolling Clwydian Hills and the foothills of Mynydd Hiraethog's moorland.

Denbigh means 'little fortress', probably referring to the original hilltop castle belonging to the ancient Welsh princes, rather than the large Norman castle you see today. After defeating the Welsh in 1282, Edward I granted the town to Henry de Lacy, who became the first Lord of Denbigh. The castle and its town walls were completed not long afterwards. The fortress would see much action in the years that followed, culminating in a successful six-month siege of Royalist troops during the Civil War. Though the castle was to fall into decay not long afterwards, there's still much to see, including the gatehouse, fronted by two polygonal towers, and walls that give tremendous views of the town, valley and the Clwydian Hills. In the

DENBIGH CASTLE

Visit

LLYN BRENIG

Llyn Brenig is a 920-acre (368ha) reservoir sited high in the superb wilderness of the Mynydd Hiraethog. Formed by the flooding of the Afon Fechan and Brenig valleys, the huge reservoir is very popular for fishing, sailing and walking. The Visitor Centre is full of useful and interesting information about the area, including its archaeological heritage. Unfortunately, some of that heritage lies beneath the water, but on the northeast shores you can discover Mesolithic camps with artefacts dating back to 5700 BC.

like Back Row thread quietly through the medieval part of the town, revealing fascinating buildings from the 15th century. The town also has the remains of a 14th-century Carmelite Friary, and the walls of an unfinished 'cathedral' dreamed up by Dudley, Earl of Leicester, one-time lover and favourite of Elizabeth I, but abandoned on his death in 1588.

Denbigh is handily placed for an exploration of the Clwydian Hills, which have long been popular with walkers who delight in the heather ridges. Moel Famau, which means 'mother mountain', is at 1,818 feet (554m) the highest of the range. Its summit monument was built in 1810 to celebrate the jubilee of King George III. The square tower and spire were wrecked by a violent gale 50 years later, and the place lay in ruins until 1970 when it was tidied up. To the west, and clearly in view from the ridge, are the concentric earthwork rings of Maes y Gaer, just one of many ancient fortifications on the range.

grounds is the 14th-century tower of the otherwise demolished St Hilary's Church and an old statue believed to be Edward I. It takes very little imagination to conjure up images of how this powerful fortress would have looked.

Beneath the castle, Denbigh has many historical corners and buildings to explore. Narrow ginnels

KNIGHTON & OFFA'S DYKE

Knighton, an attractive country market town, rather affluent in its appearance, lies on the southern bank of the River Teme, surrounded by lovely, low, rounded hills. The English border, including the town's hill, Panpunton, lies on the other side of the river. Tref y Clawdde, the Welsh name for Knighton means town on the dyke, and a motte-and-bailey castle in the heart of town stands squarely on Offa's Dyke, an 18th-century earthwork – the only place where this happens.

The main street ascends gently to a fine Victorian clock tower and then on to Market Street, with Georgian houses and businesses with traditional shopfronts, rather than the brightly coloured plastic panels of the usual high street.

Knighton has the scant remains of two castles, the open motte at Bryn-y-Castell to the east of town, and the remains of a Norman castle, sacked by Owain Glyn Dwr, which can just be seen at the back of the fire station. Both are now in private ownership. The town is an excellent base for walking, and the Offa's Dyke Centre on West Street can help with information and advice.

For centuries Welsh warlords had attacked their Anglo Saxon enemies in attempts to force them back across the Marches but, in the

Visit

RHUDDLAN CASTLE

This superb 13th-century Norman castle lies just 3 miles (5km) south of the coast at Rhyl. Those who make it to the castle on foot from the resort by following the banks of the River Clwyd, will notice that the banks are uniformly straight. The need to gain access to the fortress from the sea was satisfied by canalising the river, a huge project involving 1,800 ditchers. The powerful symmetry of the castle is very impressive, and Gillot's Tower, which provided access to the river below, and the massive twin-towered gatehouse are the dominant features.

8th century Offa, King of Mercia, decided to settle the disputes. He built a massive earthwork dyke running the full length of Wales, from Prestatyn to Chepstow, intended to mark out the political boundary of his kingdom, beyond which the Welsh were permitted only under strict control. Much of the dyke is still visible, and it more or less follows the line of the present-day dyke. The dyke in these parts is at its grandest, with clear earthwork lines straddling the moors. Today there is a well-established national trail along its length, the Offa's Dyke Path. The Glyndwr's Way, another national trail, also starts here.

Knighton is served by the Heart of Wales Railway, running from Swansea to Shrewsbury. This scenic railway weaves its way through the lonely hills and quiet valleys of beautiful Mid-Wales and is popular with walkers who want to do a linear route or those wanting to visit the Victorian spa towns of Builth and Llandrindod Wells.

121

LLANDUDNO

Llandudno is by far the most elegant of the North Wales seaside resorts. The Victorian town, whose sweeping sandy northern bay is sheltered by two great limestone promontories, Great Orme and Little Orme, also extends to a west shore looking out on to the Conwy Estuary and the mountains of Snowdonia.

The town's shopping centre is built right up to the crags of Great Orme, as is the 2,295-foot (700m) long Victorian pier, the longest and most attractive pier in Wales. Just beyond the pier visitors can take their cars up the Marine Drive toll road, which takes them on to Great Orme, where there are several well-placed car parks. The more adventurous may chose to walk to the top through a park called Happy Valley and past the ski run. Alternatively, there's a Victorian tram or a cable car. On Great Orme there's history round every corner, with Europe's only Bronze Age copper mines that are open to the public; an Iron Age fort, caves that were inhabited in the upper Palaeolithic period, and a church, St Tudno's, with 6th-century origins.

Colwyn Bay, situated on the other side of Little Orme, was established in the same Victorian era, but hasn't been blessed with Llandudno's elegance of architecture. The chief attraction here is the Welsh Mountain Zoo, overlooking Colwyn Bay, where a pair of snow leopards have been brought in from eastern Europe.

Beauty and elegance are diluted the further east you go, but they're replaced by frivolity. Rhyl, which developed into a successful resort in Victorian days, has wall-to-wall caravan parks, a pleasure beach, plenty of kiss-me-quick hats and candy floss – nice if you like that sort of thing: bedlam if you don't. The beaches are excellent and it might just be the place to keep the children happy on sunny days.

Prestatyn, the last resort before the Point of Ayre and the

Dee Estuary, has the hills for back up. Here the Clwydians come down to the sea, as does the Offa's Dyke long-distance path. In times gone by the land around here extended much further north and there are remnants of a forest, which at low tide has yielded fasinating artefacts of neolithic man.

LLANGOLLEN

The self-proclaimed gateway to Wales, Llangollen sits very prettily in the fertile and verdant Dee Valley, surrounded by the Llantysilio and Berwyn hills. The river is at the heart of the village and on any fair day you'll see scores of people congregating around the Elizabethan stone bridge, one of the Seven Wonders of Wales, seemingly mesmerised by the fast waters bursting over the riverbed rocks.

The bridge was extended in 1863 for the railway line, which linked Wrexham with Barmouth. Following the railway's closure in the 1960s, a preservation society was formed and today steam trains operate the 7.5-mile (12km) route to Carrog. The society expects that it will eventually re-open the line to Corwen.

Llangollen station is an evocative reminder of days gone by, with its historic steam engines and rolling stock lined up on platforms that are spanned by the original Great Western region footbridge.

The Llangollen canal runs parallel to the railway and road. Pioneered by Thomas Telford, it provides another transport leisure link for horse-drawn narrowboats, which take visitors along the canal and over the Pontcysyllte Aqueduct, where a cast-iron trough carries the canal for 1,007 feet (300m), 120 feet (35m) above the River Dee.

Looking to the skies you can see the ruffled outlines of castle ruins perched on a limestone knoll above the town. Known as Dinas Bran, it was occupied by the Princes of Powys. A walk up the hill reveals that the ruins are quite extensive and the views up the Dee Valley are

Visit

MONTGOMERY

Montgomery ticks over at an altogether more leisurely pace than Welshpool. This fine country town has an elegant red-brick town hall with a clock tower, and a half-timbered 16th-century inn, the Dragon Hotel, is dominated by its medieval castle, established by William I's friend, Roger de Montgomery. The huge earthworks of the Fridd Faldwyn fort were built long before the Roman Conquest. Artefacts, including neolithic tools, are now held in the National Museum in Cardiff.

tremendous – they're far better than the famed Horseshoe Pass, a 4-mile (6km) drive away. Behind Dinas Bran are the long tiered limestone cliffs of Creigiau Eglwyseg. One of the most impressive sights of the region, they stretch to a place called World's End!

Just off the A542 Horseshoe Pass road in the deep, narrow Eglwyseg Valley, lies the ruined abbey of Valle Crucis, a name that means valley of the cross. This was a reference to the cross that used to top the Pillar of Eliseg, a memorial to the 9th-century Prince of Powys. Established in 1201 by Cistercian monks from Strata Marcella near Welshpool, the abbey is sited in fertile pastures beneath a knoll delightfully named the Velvet Hill.

WELSHPOOL

Set amid Montgomeryshire's rolling verdant hills and wide valley of the River Severn, Welshpool, Y Trallwng to give it its Welsh name, has over the centuries become a prosperous and bustling market town. Until 1835 it was known as Pool; some of the old mileposts still refer to it in that way. The Welsh translation was added to distinguish the place from Poole in Dorset. It was the Severn that brought trade to the town, for it was navigable by boat. The Montgomery Canal came to the town in 1797, part of a 33-mile (53km) system from Welsh Frankton in Shropshire to Newtown in Powys.

It was built by three different companies and opened in stages. It was designed for narrowboats, but today it is a quiet backwater and a pleasant place for a stroll. The lack of recent activity on the canal has allowed several interesting plant species to grow, including water plantain and frogbit. Today's visitor can find out much more at the Powysland Museum and Montgomery Canal Centre, where there is a V-shaped basin used as a winding point and as a base for the Montgomery Canal Cruises.

The pride of Welshpool's town centre is its High Street, a thoroughfare of fine architecture, much dating from the Georgian era, like the Royal Oak Hotel, but many much older half-timbered buildings, such as the Talbot Hotel and numbers 8–11 belong to the 16th century. A building with a more dubious past is the Cockpit on New Street, which would have been the popular venue for cockfights until the ban in 1849.

Almost every tourist who comes to Welshpool comes to see Powis Castle, which was built for the warring Princes of Powys in around 1200. A long drive from Park Lane off the High Street leads through the fine estate's parklands, past mature oaks and grazing deer to reach the castle. Because of its continuous occupation since 1578, when the ownership passed to the Herbert family, the old fortress has become more of a mansion, with castellated ramparts, tall chimneys, rows of fine leaded windows and fine 17th-century balustraded terraces overlooking manicured lawns and neatly clipped yews. Lead statues of a shepherd and shepherdess survive and keep watch over the many shrubs and perennial borders.

For those wanting to explore the Montgomeryshire hills even further, the Welshpool and Llanfair Light Railway, can take you on an interesting journey through the picturesque and verdant Banwy Valley to Llanfair Caereinion.

TOURIST INFORMATION CENTRES

Knighton
Offa's Dyke Centre, West Street.
Tel: 01547 529 424

Llandudno
1–2 Chapel Street.
Tel: 01492 876 413

Llangollen
Castle Street.
Tel: 01978 860 828

Welshpool
Vicarage Gardens.
Tel: 01938 552043

PLACES OF INTEREST

Alice in Wonderland Centre
3 & 4 Trinity Square, Llandudno.
Tel: 01492 860082;
www.wonderland.co.uk
Life-size displays of the Lewis Carroll,
Alice in Wonderland story and its
connections to Llandudno.

Chirk Castle
Chirk, Nr Wrexham.
Tel: 01691 777701

Denbigh Castle
Tel: 01745 813385

Great Orme Mines
Great Orme, Llandudno.
Tel: 01492 870447
Fascinating Bronze Age copper mines.

Llangollen Steam Railway
Abbey Road, Llangollen.
Tel: 01978 860951 (timetable);
www.llangollen-railway.co.uk

Llangollen Wharf
Llangollen.
Tel: 01978 860702;
www.horsedrawnboats.co.uk
For horse-drawn narrowboat canal
trips over the great Telford aqueduct
and Froncysyllte.

Powis Castle
Welshpool.
Tel: 01938 551944
Medieval castle with a fine collection of
paintings.

Powysland Museum and Canal Centre
The Canal Wharf, Welshpool.
Tel: 01938 554656
Housed in a refurbished canal-side
warehouse, the museum illustrates the
history of Montgomeryshire including
its canal.

Rhuddlan Castle
Near Rhyl.
Tel: 01745 590777

Rhyl Sky Tower
Rhyl Promenade.
A 240-foot (73m) modern tower whose
observation car rotates to give birds'
eye views of the North Wales Coast.

Welshpool and Llanfair Light Railway
The Station, Llanfair Caereinion.
Tel: 01938 810441; www.wllr.org.uk
Narrow-gauge steam railway between
Welshpool and Llanfair Caereinion.

FOR CHILDREN
Harlequin Puppet Theatre
Rhos on Sea Promenade, Colwyn Bay.
Tel: 01492 548166
Britain's only permanent marionette
theatre.

Rhyl Sun Centre
East Parade, Rhyl.
Tel: 01745 344433
An indoor tropical water park, with
'white rollers' to surf and daredevil
waterslides to scare.

SeaQuarium
Promenade, Rhyl.
Tel: 01745 344660;
www.seaquarium.co.uk

SHOPPING
Market Days
Colwyn Bay, Tue and Sat; farmers'
market, Thu.
Denbigh, Wed.
Knighton, Thu.
Llangollen, Tue.
Prestatyn, Tue, Fri, Sat.
Ruthin, Thu.
Welshpool, Mon
Wrexham, Mon.

PERFORMING ARTS
Clwyd Theatre
Mold. Tel: 0845 330 3565

Theatr Colwyn
Abergele Rd, Colwyn Bay.
Tel: 01492 532668

Venue Cymru
Promenade, Llandudno.
Tel: 01492 872000;
www.venuecymru.co.uk

SPORTS & ACTIVITIES

ANGLING

Shore Fishing

Llandudno, Colwyn Bay, Rhos, Deganwy, Rhyl, Mostyn Docks.

FLY FISHING

Llyn Brenig.

Fly fishing lake filled with rainbow trout. Permits from The Visitor Centre, Brenig Reservoir, Cerrigydrudion.
Tel: 01490 420463
Day permits from machines.

BEACHES

Abergele

A good beach popular with windsurfers and canoeists. Good car parking.

Colwyn Bay

A lively pier and a good arcing sandy beach sheltered by the Little Orme.

Llandudno

Two excellent sandy beaches either side of the Great Orme. The West Beach has a pier and many activities like Punch and Judy shows.

Prestatyn

4 miles (6.5km) of sand, very popular with families.

Rhyl

3 miles (5km) of sand, good for families.

CYCLING

There's a traffic-free ride along the promenade from Rhos-on-Sea (nr Colwyn Bay) to Prestatyn (16 miles/26km – one way), and a 9-mile (14.5km) circuit at Llyn Brenig Reservoir near Denbigh. Also a trip around Lake Vyrnwy on quiet lanes.

GOLF

Information available from www.visitwales.co.uk

Chirk Golf Club

Chirk, Nr Wrexham.
Tel: 01691 774407. 18 holes.

Knighton Golf Club

Ffrydd Wood, Knighton.
Tel: 01547 528046. 9 holes.

Llanymynech Golf Club

Pant, Nr Oswestry.
Tel: 01691 830983. 18 holes.

Old Colwyn Golf Club

Woodland Avenue, Old Colwyn.
Tel: 01492 515581
9 holes.

Rhos-on-Sea Golf Club
Glan-y-mor Road, Penrhyn Bay,
Llandudno.
Tel: 01492 549641. 18 holes.

HORSE-RIDING

J S Pughe
Pont-y-Meibion, Pandy, Glyn Ceiriog,
Llangollen, LL20 7HS.
Tel: 01691 718413

Mill Pony Trekking
Llwycoed Mill, Bwlch Y Ffridd,
Newtown, Powys, SY16 3JE.
Tel: 01686 688440

Ruthin Riding Centre
Ruthin, LL15 2YE.
Tel: 01824 703470

Sychdyn Riding Centre
Tai Cochion, Greenbank Lane,
Sychdyn, Mold, Clwyd.
Tel: 01352 840284

Tynllwyn Riding Stables
Tynllwyn Farm, Brynymaen, Colwyn
Bay. Tel: 01492 580224

SKIING
Llandudno Ski and Snowboard Centre
Wyddfyd, Great Orme, Llandudno.
Tel: 01492 874707;
www.llandudnoskislope.co.uk

WALKING

Long Distance Routes
Offa's Dyke Path (Chepstow to
Prestatyn).
Good walking opportunities on
Clwydian Hills, Loggerheads Country
Park and the Berwyn Hills.

WATERSPORTS

Canoeing and Rafting
JJ Canoeing and Rafting,
Mile End Mill, Berwyn Road,
Llangollen.
Tel: 01978 860736;
www.jjraftcanoe.com
Llangollen activity centre.

ANNUAL FESTIVALS & EVENTS

Flintshire
Flintshire Festival, Oct. Drama, dance
and music. Tel: 01352 702472

Llangollen
International Eisteddfod, early Jul.
Music dance and culture.
Tel: 01978 862000

Ruthin
Ruthin Festival, Jun/Jul.
Music festival.
Tel: 01824 703832

133

TEA ROOMS

Badgers Café and Patisserie
The Victoria Centre, Mostyn Street,
Llandudno, LL30 2RP
Tel: 01492 871649

Here, delicious teas, coffees and cream cakes are served by Victorian-style waitresses known as Badgers' Nippies. Welsh treats such as bara brith and Welsh cakes are on the menu, along with Welsh rarebit, swan meringues and dragon eclairs.

The Buttery
8 High Street, Welshpool, SY21 7JP
Tel: 01938 552658

Set in a gorgeous black-and-white timbered building dating back to the early 16th century, this friendly café is open daily for a wide variety of snacks and meals. Families are welcome with children's menus and smaller portions available. Vegetarians can enjoy dishes, such as Stilton, broccoli and mushroom lasagne.

Honey Pots Ceramic Café
18 Castle Street,
Llangollen, LL20 8NU
Tel: 01978 869008
www.honey-pots.com

At Honey Pots you can enjoy delicious teas or coffees and tasty cakes and snacks in smart modern surroundings while admiring the views of Dinas Bran's hilltop castle. When you have had your fill of cakes you can turn your hand to designing your own, unique piece of pottery.

Britannia Inn
**Horseshoe Pass, Llangollen,
LL20 8DW. Tel: 01978 860144**
The popular 14th-century inn built by
the monks of nearby Valle Crucis is at
the foot of the Horseshoe Pass with
views over the Vale of Llangollen. The
cosy inn has open fires and beamed
ceilings and serves Theakston's ales
and a good selection of bar meals. .

Dragon Hotel
**Montgomery, SY15 6PA
Tel: 01686 668359
www.dragonhotel.com**
The impressive half-timbered coaching
inn offers an extensive menu with
blackboard specials. You'll find local
produce including lamb and beef,
vegetarian options, tasty pasta and
game dishes. The beers are from the
local Wood brewery and Boddingtons.

Grouse Inn
**Carrog, Corwen, LL21 9AT
Tel: 01490 430272**
Enjoy views across the Dee and the
Vale of Llangollen to the Berwyn
Mountains. It's just a short walk from
Carrog station on the Llangollen Steam
Line. Excellent cask ales are served
along with good food and specials.

Hawk & Buckle Inn
**Llannefydd, Denbigh, LL16 5ED
Tel: 01745 540249**
The 17th-century coaching inn, situated
high up in the hills, is well known for its
fine cuisine and welcoming ambience.
There is an extensive menu, which
uses local lamb, beef and salmon. A
creative bar menu includes vegetarian
options. Children are welcome.

West Arms
**Llanarmon, Dyffryn Ceiriog, LL20 7LD
Tel: 01691 600665**
The West Arms is cosy and welcoming
with its beamed ceilings and roaring
log fires. Thanks to renowned chef
Grant Williams the cuisine is of
international standard with dishes such
as steamed local breast of pheasant
wrapped in leeks with a confit of wild
mushrooms laced in a delicious truffle-
scented sauce.

137

Brecon Beacons
& Mid Wales

INTRODUCTION

Four great mountain ranges, the Black Mountain in the west, Fforest Fawr, the Brecon Beacons and the Black Mountains of the east, form the spine of the National Park' and many of the sandstone escarpments have finely sculpted northern cliffs and instantly recognisable table-like summits. The Brecon Beacons valleys are fertile, with fields as green and lush as those of Ireland, but to the north the scenery transforms into the wild remote hills and valleys of Mid Wales, a haven for those in seach of some peace and quiet.

HOT SPOTS

Unmissable attractions

Walk, climb or just stand and gaze across the Brecon Beacons' fertile valleys, with fields as green and lush as those of Ireland, or the wild remote hills and valleys of Mid Wales, a haven for those who like tranquillity and a more subtle beauty...explore Hay-on-Wye, a vibrant market town with a rich history, bookshops galore and an annual literary festival...get into the swing at the jazz festival in Brecon...cycle around the Elan Valley, an easy route along an old railway trackbed...visit the fascinating Centre for Alternative Technology in a disused Llwyngwern slate quarry.

2

1 Hay-on-Wye

The beautiful Wye Valley, including the stretch around Hay-on-Wye, is worthy of exploration.

2 Llandovery

A delightfully lush green countryside with rolling hills between Llandovery and the Brecon Beacons.

3 Elan Valley
The mighty Victorian dam of the Craig Goch reservoir holds back the waters of the Elan Valley.

4 Aberystwyth
Aberystwyth, set on the sweeping golden sands of Cardigan Bay, is the main seaside town of Mid Wales.

5 Brecon Beacons
Walking is the most popular activity in the Brecon Beacons with more than 620 miles (1,000km) of rights of way.

5

ABERYSTWYTH

ABERYSTWYTH & CEREDIGION COAST

Seen from the pier, Aberystwyth, the largest resort on Cardigan Bay, looks like any other British seaside town, with a pleasant arc of dark sand and pebble beach, neat rows of Victorian hotels and B&Bs, and a nice green hill at the far end. But it is a town of great historical importance and with more than a little culture.

In the 6th century, Celtic missionaries set up a monastery at Llanbadarn, the original name for Aberystwyth, but the concentric rings of an ancient hill fort on the summit of Penparcau, clearly visible from the harbour, date back to 600 BC. Over the centuries the religious settlement developed into a centre of learning, one that continues today with the university and the Library of Wales. Like most strategic places in Wales the town has its Norman castle, though this one is in ruins after it was blown up in 1649, just six years after it served as a Royal Mint for Charles II.

147

Many visitors take the short ride on the cliff railway to Constitution Hill, where there is café, a camera obscura, and a superb view of Aberystwyth and the whole of the Cardigan Bay coastline.

The Vale of Rheidol narrow-gauge railway, built in 1902, takes passengers on an hour-long journey to Devil's Bridge, revealing spectacular views of the wooded Rheidol Valley along the way.

At Devil's Bridge coin-operated turnstiles either side of the road allow access to paths into a spectacular wooded gorge where you'll see three bridges, one on top of another (legend has it that the lowest one was built with the help of the Devil) and the Mynach Falls, which tumble from a great height past the treetops into the depths of the gorge far beneath your feet.

Further to the south along the coast from Aberystwyth are the pretty resorts of Aberaeron and Newquay. Aberaeron, a more sedate resort ideal for coast-walkers, has stylish colour-washed Georgian terraces overlooking the quay and riverside, while the busy but pretty seaside town of Newquay is ideal for families with its sandy beach.

To the north of Aberystwyth, bordering the Dyfi Estuary lies the peat bogs of Cors Fochno, an important National Nature Reserve.

Visit

PLYNLIMON

Plynlimon Fawr (Pumlumon in Welsh) is one of the country's three principle mountains – the other two are Snowdon and Cadair Idris. George Borrow, a 19th-century writer loved the mountain, and sipped the water from the sources of its three great rivers, the Severn, the Wye and the Rheidol. Two corners of this wild mountain that are well worth visiting are the lake filled rocky corrie of Llyn Llygad Rheidol to the north of the main summit, and Glaslyn, a high windswept lake accessible by car from the Machynlleth–Llanidloes mountain road.

ABERGAVENNY

Abergavenny, which is by far the largest town in the upper Usk Valley, occupies a large basin surrounded by three very distinctly shaped mountains: the cone-shaped Sugar Loaf Mountain and the craggy Ysgyryd Fawr in the north; Blorenge in the south. It's also well situated as a base to explore the Black Mountains and the Brecon Beacons.

Although it took a pounding after the Civil War, Abergavenny's Norman castle is still worth seeing, as is the interesting museum next door. There's no shortage of castles in the surrounding area too. Raglan lies just 10 miles (16km) east along the A40, while the lesser known 'three castles' of Grosmont, Skenfrith and White Castle are hidden away in low, rolling hills a few miles to the east.

Along some of the narrowest country lanes imaginable in the beautiful Vale of Ewyas, lie the romantic ruins of Llanthony Priory founded by Augustinian canons early in the 12th century.

For visitors who find Abergavenny a little too busy – they do get traffic jams here – Crickhowell, further west up the Usk Valley, is a picturesque village that is almost as well sited for many of the tourist attractions in the area.

BRECON & PEN Y FAN

Although the Romans made their home here, Brecon's roots date back to the 5th century when it was governed by the Celtic chieftain, Brychan, who gave his name to the town. Situated at the confluences of the rivers Usk, Honddu and Tarell, the town grew rapidly in importance during Norman times when a Benedictine monastery, a castle and formidable town walls were built. In the Act of Union of 1536 Brecon was listed as one of four local capitals and in 1542 Henry VIII set up a chancery here, installing the exchequer in the castle.

Modern Brecon sees the castle as no more than a battlemented wall set in the gardens of the Castle of

Brecon Hotel, while only fragments of the town wall still stand near Captains Walk.

St John's Church, part of the monastery, survived Henry VIII's Dissolution of Monasteries and in 1923 was elevated to cathedral status. The impressive old, red sandstone building was extensively refurbished in 1872 by Sir Gilbert Scott, whose finest work is the chancel's vaulted ceiling.

Visit

WATERFALL COUNTRY

Four streams, the Nedd, Pyrddin, Mellte and Hepste tumble down from the moors of Fforest Fawr to cut deep gorges through the more permeable limestone rocks. They create a series of spectacular waterfalls in the woods north of Pontneddfechan. All are approachable by footpath from car parks just south of the tiny village of Ystradfellte. At the most impressive fall, Sgwd yr Eira, visitors can walk behind the falls and look through the cascading water.

The town centre's buildings are a mixture of Georgian, Jacobean and Tudor, with a network of narrow streets leading off the Bulwark. The 19th-century Shire Hall with its Athenian-style columns, houses the lively and fascinating Brecknock Museum and Art Gallery, while Brecon's military history is well-recorded and celebrated at the Museums of the Royal Regiment of Wales in the Barracks.

Each August, Brecon swings to its own jazz festival, one of Britain's premier jazz events. For those who like old steam railways, the Brecon Mountain Railway puffs 7 miles (11km) from Pant just north of Merthyr Tydfil, into the foothills of the Brecon Beacons.

Seemingly always in view from the town and river banks, the Beacons' twin peaks, Pen y Fan (2,907ft/886m) and Corn Du (2,863ft/873m) display their angular outlines, finely sculpted northern cliffs and shadowy cwms to perfection. The proliferation of

walking gear shops in the town shows that many visitors come to walk and there's no finer place than Brecon to explore southern Britain's highest mountains.

GLYNTAWE & UPPER SWANSEA VALLEY

The transition from stark industrial landscapes to rural ones happens very suddenly in the Swansea Valley. One minute you're in Ystradgynlais on the edge of the old coalfields, the next you've turned the corner past Abercraf into the magical garden-like landscapes of Glyntawe and you're staring across the River Tawe up to the limestone crags of Cribarth, a southern outlier of the Black Mountain. Glyntawe, a sprawling village, is one of the best starting points for a climb on the Fan Hir escarpment to the highest Black Mountain summit, Fan Brycheiniog.

The limestone geology of the valley has left it with its major attraction, the Dan yr Ogof Caves, discovered in 1912. This is Wales' largest subterranean cavern system, where visitors can enter a weird world of impressive stalactites, stalagmites and underground waterfalls brought to life with lighting and music. The south side of the valley is dominated by Craig y Nos Castle, once home to world famous Victorian opera singer Adelina Patti. This Gothic mansion, now a grand hotel, is surrounded by superb riverside gardens with mature woodland fringing meres and meadows that now form a valuable part of the Craig y Nos Country Park.

HAY-ON-WYE

Hay-on-Wye lies in the northeast corner of the Brecon Beacons National Park by the sleepy banks of the River Wye, and sheltered by the sweeping slopes of the Black Mountains. With the flower-decked meadows and rolling green hills of Radnorshire in the north, spring and summer in Hay are delightful times.

The name 'hay' comes from the Norman word *haie* meaning

'enclosed place'. It's known that there was a settlement here when King Offa of Mercia built his dyke here in the 8th century. There are only fragmented remains of the old Norman town walls in the Newport Street area, but this would have been a heavily fortified border town since the 13th century when William de Breos built his castle. The baron soon fell out with King John and was forced to flee to France, where he died in poverty; it's believed that after sacking the castle King John's men starved the baron's wife and child to death. Further attacks and destruction came at the hands of Llewelyn the Great and Owain Glyn Dwr, and by fire as late as 1977.

Today Hay is a vibrant market town known for its 30-plus second-hand and antiquarian bookshops and tourists come from all over the world to visit the annual literary festival. Among a maze of narrow streets you'll discover many fascinating old buildings, including a colonnaded 19th-century butter market, the 16th-century Three Tuns pub, which still has its horse-mounting block outside, and a splendid Victorian clock tower.

Visit

LLANTHONY PRIORY

A delightful little road climbs south from Hay over the Gospel Pass before descending deeply into the beautiful Vale of Ewyas, where the romantic ruins of Llanthony Priory bask in the beauty of pasture, lovely hedgerows, dense woodland and the impressive backdrop of the Black Mountains.

The Augustinian Priory was established in 1103 by the son of a Marcher lord, William de Lacey. After a viscious attack by Owain Glyn Dwr the priory was left ruinous, but there are still substantial amount of the building to explore, including arches, walls and towers. he ruins won't fail to impress and stir the imagination. Unusually, you can enjoy the fine view over a pie and a pint, as there's a pub in the grounds.

Visit

THE DINAS NATURE RESERVE

This RSPB reserve, which lies 10 miles (16km) north of Llandovery and south of Llyn Brianne, has a footpath over wetlands and through oak woodland to the steep slopes of Dinas. There's a cave in the crags here, where Twm Sion Catti, the Welsh Robin Hood, used to hide from his enemies. Red kites can often be seen soaring above the trees and in summer, you can also see dippers, pied flycatchers, common sandpipers and grey wagtails.

LLANDOVERY & TYWI VALLEY

Llandovery, known here as Llanymyddfri – 'the church amongst the waters' – was described by the 19th-century writer, George Borrow, as 'the pleasantest little town in which I have halted in the course of my wanderings'. The area was once occupied by the Romans, whose fort, Alabum, was sited near to St Mary's Church by the Afon Bran to the north of the town. The castle, which was built for the Norman baron Richard Fitz Pons in the 12th century, was captured by the Welsh in the Glyn Dwr Revolts. In 1532 its owner, Rhys-ap-Gruffydd, was executed at the hands of Henry VIII for treason and, in an act of revenge by the Welsh, the castle was destroyed, never to be rebuilt. A recently erected statue of Llewelyn ap Grufydd stands guard on the grassy bank beneath the remains of the castle keep. Across the car park from the statue you'll find the Heritage Centre where you can get information about walks in the area, and discover the myths and history of the region.

Llandovery's history is intertwined with the fortunes of the cattle drovers. When thieves made travelling on Wales' rugged roads a hazardous exercise, the local farmers hired the drovers to drive cattle to the more lucrative markets of England and to settle accounts for them with non-local people. This meant that drovers needed to handle

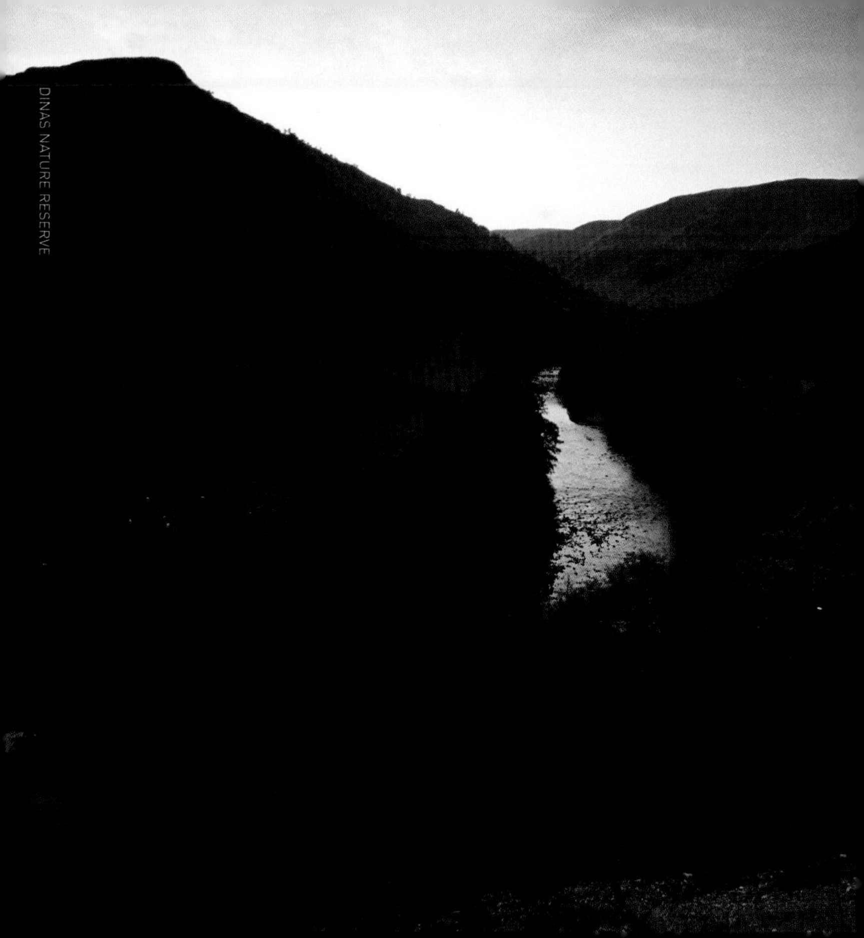

DINAS NATURE RESERVE

Visit

ALTERNATIVE TECHNOLOGY

The Centre for Alternative Technology was founded in 1973 and utilised the disused Llwyngwern slate quarry, a couple of miles (3.2km) north of Machynlleth. From very small beginnings, the centre now has a workforce of 90 permanent staff and volunteers on the 7-acre (2.8ha) site. Visitors to the centre can get up the hill on an amazing water-powered cliff railway. They will see exciting interactive displays about global issues such as energy generation and transport, along with some practical ideas for their own homes and lifestyles, including organic gardening.

large sums of money and led to the introduction of banking systems some of them even issuing bank notes. One of the most successful of these was David Jones' Black Ox Bank, which was taken over at the turn of the 20th century by Lloyds.

To the south of Llandovery, the Black Mountain (or Mynydd Du as it is known in Wales) lies at the western end of the Brecon Beacon Range, rising in grand escarpments of old red sandstone. Glacial action has formed magnificent cliffs on the northern and eastern faces of the group and also provided two lovely tarns: Llyn y Fan Fawr and Llyn y Fan Fach. Myddfai, which is sheltered in the northern foothills of the Black Mountain, is a picturesque village with a fine 13th-century church and splendid country pub, the Plough.

MACHYNLLETH

Machynlleth shelters on high ground to the south of the wide valley of the Dyfi, where the mountains of Snowdonia give way to the rolling foothills of Plynlimon. A fine 17th-century four-arched stone bridge spans the river on the road leading into this small market town. An 80-foot (24m) Victorian clock tower of an extremely ornate design forms the hub of this town centre and looks down on a wide Maengwyn Street, where the weekly Wednesday markets are held. Here you'll also find Parliament House, a medieval town house standing on the site where Owain Glyn Dwr held the last independent Welsh Parliament in 1404. It now hosts an Owain Glyn Dwr interpretative centre. The early 14th-century Royal House at the junction of Garsiwn Lane and Penrallt Street is so called because Charles I stayed here in 1644.

Plas Machynlleth, and its parklands, which lie between Maengwyn Street and the hills to the south, is a mansion built between the 17th and 19th centuries for the Marquis of Londonderry and his descendants. The property was left to the town on the 7th Marquess' death in 1948 and now houses the fascinating Celtica heritage centre.

Today Machynlleth has an appealing mix of all things Welsh, Celtic mysticism, and green idealism. The unusual shops and the wholefood café are a testament to this, as is the Centre for Alternative Technology. The townsfolk were a bit

Insight

THE PHYSICIANS OF MYDDFAI

Llyn y Fan Fach at the northern foot of the Black Mountain is an eerie place and it's not surprising that there's some mystery and legend lurking beneath its waters. From its depths a flaxen-haired fairy appeared and enchanted a local farmer's boy, Rhiwallon. After altercations with her husband the fairy returned to the waters. However, the couple sired three sons, who would learn from their mother about medicine. The boys became the first in a line of Physicians of Myddfai, the last was Dr C Rice Williams of Aberystwyth, who died in 1842.

dubious when the 'hippies' first set up the alternative living centre, but their fortunes are now intertwined.

RHANDIRMWYN

Once an important old lead-mining village, Rhandirmwyn lies in the valley of the Upper Tywi, 9 miles (14km) north of Llandovery and the

LLYN BRIANNE

A40. This is a haven for those who like riverside walks, angling and birding. Two fine bird reserves are set scenically among the attractive riverside crags, where the boisterous Tywi and Doethie rivers twist and turn between rocky, oak-clad peaks. Beneath the conical hill called Dinas, the rivers converge in a violent cauldron of foam.

Just a short distance upstream, where the Doethie River meets up with the Pysgotwr River, is one of the wildest gorges in Mid Wales. Just a few miles north of Rhandirmwyn along winding country lanes, Llyn Brianne Reservoir is surrounded by plantations of spruce and larch in two narrow valleys, those of the Tywi and Camddwr.

RHAYADER

Rhayader's full Welsh name is Rhaeadr Gwy, meaning 'waterfall on the Wye'. The waterfall to which it refers was actually blown up in 1780 to make way for a much-needed bridge over the river.

163

Visit

GIGRIN FARM

Gigrin Farm, an upland sheep farm on the A470, 0.6 mile (1km) south of Rhayader, is an official RSPB feeding station for red kites. It's fascinating to see first the noisy crows arriving on the scene, then the red kites and buzzards swooping down at break-neck speed to foil the smaller birds. The number of kites visiting the feeding station can vary from a dozen to around 400 or so. Feeding the birds takes place every afternoon.

Dominated by its opulent Victorian clock tower, which lies at the crossroads in the centre of the village, Rhayader is a very pleasant town set among some of the finest river scenery in Mid Wales. The poet Percy Shelley was drawn to these parts in 1809. He lived in the cottage of Nantgwyllt in the Elan Valley, then a famed beauty spot. However, the planned flooding of the Elan Valley was to change the nature of the scenery forever. In the first part of the scheme, four reservoirs, the Craig Goch, Penygarreg, Carreg-ddu and Caban-coch were constructed. Nantgwyllt was among the dwellings submerged by the reservoirs. Its garden walls can still be seen when Caban-coch's water levels are low. A church, chapel, school and numerous farms were submerged when the scheme was completed in 1904. A fifth reservoir, the Claerwen, was completed in 1952. One hundred years later the reservoirs have blended almost seamlessly with their surroundings and the power of the dams, and the white waters thundering down them, adds great character to the landscape. The visitor centre gives an intriguing insight into the construction of the dams, the railway built to supply them and the lives of the construction workers involved in the project. The old railway trackbed now forms the Elan Valley Trail, which is a marvellous facility for waterside walking or cycling.

ELAN VALLEY

TOURIST INFORMATION CENTRES

Aberystwyth
Terrace Road.
Tel: 01970 612125

Brecon
Cattle Market Car Park.
Tel: 01874 622485

Hay-on-Wye
Oxford Road.
Tel: 01497 820144

Llandrindod Wells
Old Town Hall, Memorial Gardens.
Tel: 01597 822600

Llanidloes
54 Longbridge Street.
Tel: 01686 412605

Machynlleth
Canolfan Owain Glyndwr.
Tel: 01654 702401

Rhayader
The Leisure Centre, North Street.
Tel: 01597 810591

PLACES OF INTEREST

Brecon Cathedral
Cathedral Close, Brecon, Powys.
Tel: 01874 623857

Carreg Cennen Castle
Trapp, Nr Llandeilo.
Tel: 01558 822291. Perhaps Wales'
most spectacularly sited castle on high
cliffs overlooking the Tywi Valley.

Centre for Alternative Technology
Machynlleth. Tel: 01654 705950;
www.cat.org.uk
See some of the solutions to the
challenges facing Earth.

**Ceredigion Museum and Coliseum
Gallery**
Coliseum,Terrace Road, Aberystwyth,
Dyfed.
Tel: 01970 633088
A fine collection of historic objects
including the furniture, archaeology,
agriculture, seafaring and lead mining
industries of the people of Ceredigion.

Dan-yr-Ogof Showcaves
Brecon Rd, Penycae.
Tel: 01639 730284;
www.dan-yr-ogof-showcaves.co.uk
Visit the underground world of
stalagmites, stalactites, waterfalls, a
museum and the dinosaur park.

Dinas Nature Reserve
Rhandirmwyn.
RSPB reserve with beautiful walk and
shop/information centre. Charge for
car park.

Dolaucothi Gold Mines
Pumpsaint, Llanwrda
Carmarthenshire.
(Site off A482 between Lampeter and
Llanwrda.)
Tel: 01558 650177
Free for National Trust members
(excludes underground tour).
The only known Roman gold mine in
Britain.

Gigrin Farm Kite Feeding Station
South St, Rhayader.
Tel: 01597 810243
See the rare bird of prey, the red kite.

National Cycle Collection
The Automobile Palace, Temple Street,
Llandrindod Wells. Tel: 01597 825531;
www.cyclemuseum.org.uk
Boneshakers, penny farthings and
modern bikes.

National Library of Wales
Penglais, Aberystwyth.
Tel: 01970 623816. Includes exhibitions,
cinema and a restaurant.

FOR CHILDREN
Brecon Mountain Railway
Pant Station, Merthyr Tydfil.
Tel: 01685 722988;
www.breconmountainrailway.co.uk
A narrow-gauge steam line.

Vale of Rheidol Railway
Park Avenue, Aberystwyth.
Tel: 01970 625819;
www.rheidolrailway.co.uk
One of the Great Little Trains of Wales.

SHOPPING
Market Days
Abergavenny, Tue; Farmers market, 4th Thu of month.
Aberaeron, Farmers Market, Sat.
Aberystwyth, 3rd Sat of the month.
Brecon, Tue and Fri.
Cardigan, Farmers market, first Thu of month, Apr–Dec.
Hay-on-Wye, Thu.
Lampeter, alternate Tue.
Llandrindod Wells, Fri; farmers market last Thu am of the month.
Llanidloes, Sat.
Machynlleth, Wed.

PERFORMING ARTS
Aberystwyth Arts Centre
The University of Wales, Aberystwyth, Penglais Campus, Aberystwyth.
Tel: 01970 622882
The Tabernacle
Penrallt St, Machynlleth, Powys.
Tel: 01654 703355
Theatr Brycheiniog
Canal Wharf, Brecon.
Tel: 01874 611622

Theatr Hafren
Llanidloes Rd, Newtown, SY16 4HX.
Tel: 01686 625007

SPORTS & ACTIVITIES
ANGLING
Freshwater
Numerous opportunities for fishing on farms, lakes and rivers, including the Clwydog Reservoir near Llanidloes, the Beacons Reservoir at the head of the Taff Valley and the River Tawe in Carmarthenshire. Permits and licences are available from tackle shops and TICs.
BOAT TRIPS
New Quay Boat Company
Newquay. Tel: 07989 175124
Pleasure and fishing trips.
CYCLING
Cycle Routes
Taff Trail (Cardiff to Brecon Beacons).
Shore of Llangors (Lake).
Elan Valley Trail (Rhayader to Elan Reservoirs).

GOLF

Borth & Ynys Golf Club
Aer y Mor, Borth.
Tel: 01970 871202
18 holes.

Cradoc Golf Club
Penoyre Park, Cradoc, Brecon.
Tel: 01874 623658
18 holes.

Machynlleth Golf Club
Newtown Rd, Machynlleth.
Tel: 01654 702000. 9 holes.

Rhosgoch Golf & Leisure Club
Rhosgoch, Builth Wells.
Tel: 01544 370286
18 holes.

St Idloes Golf Club
Trefeglwys Rd, Llanidloes.
Tel: 01686 412559

HORSE-RIDING

Cantref Riding Centre
Cantref, Brecon.
Tel: 01874 665223;
www.cantref.com

Mills Bros
New Court, Felindre, Three Cocks,
Brecon.
Tel: 01497 847285

Taliesin Riding Centre
Erglodd, Taliesin, Machynlleth.
Tel: 01970 832215

Underhill Riding Stables
Underhill Farm, Dolau, Llandrindod
Wells. Tel: 01597 851890

WALKING

Long-Distance Routes
The Beacons Way.
Glyndwr's Way.

ANNUAL CUSTOMS & EVENTS

Aberystwyth
Musicfest, end Jul.
www.aberfest.com

Brecon
Jazz festival, mid Aug.
Tel: 01874 625557;
www.breconjazz.co.uk

Builth Wells
Royal Welsh Show, mid to end Jul.
Agricultural show.
Tel: 01982 553683

Hay
Hay Festival, end May to early Jun.
Literary festival
Tel: 01497 821217l;
www.hayfestival.co.uk

TEA ROOMS

Giglios Coffee Shop
10 Bethel Square,
Brecon, LD3 7JP
Tel: 01874 625062

A modern licensed coffee shop and restaurant in the heart of Brecon. Excellent cream teas, gateaux and sandwiches, such as smoked salmon and cream cheese, Thai green chicken, or salmon with dill mayonnaise. A wide variety of teas and coffees is on offer.

The Granary
20, Broad Street,
Hay-on-Wye, HR3 5DB
Tel: 01497 820790

The splendid licensed café has a cosy bistro style interior with outside tables looking across to the town's Victorian clocktower. Food includes sandwiches, jacket potatoes and warming soups as well as full main meals.

Nant y Bai Mill
Rhandirmwyn,
Llandovery, SA20 0PB
Tel: 01550 760211

A wonderfully situated country café/restaurant/B&B in the beautiful Tywi Valley, the old mill serves light lunches (sandwiches, jacket potatoes, Welsh rarebit), afternoon teas and excellent evening meals in a cosy atmosphere. Choices on the menu may include the likes of guinea fowl, cooked with fresh herbs and vegetables, and local rabbit braised in white wine and Dijon mustard sauce. Book in advance for evening dining.

The Quarry Shop and Café
Maengwyn Street,
Machynlleth, SY20 8EB
Tel: 01654 702624

A very popular whole food vegetarian café set up by the Centre for Alternative Technology. They only use seasonal, organic and Fair Trade produce. Their date slices are absolutely delicious and the soups will warm you on cold days.

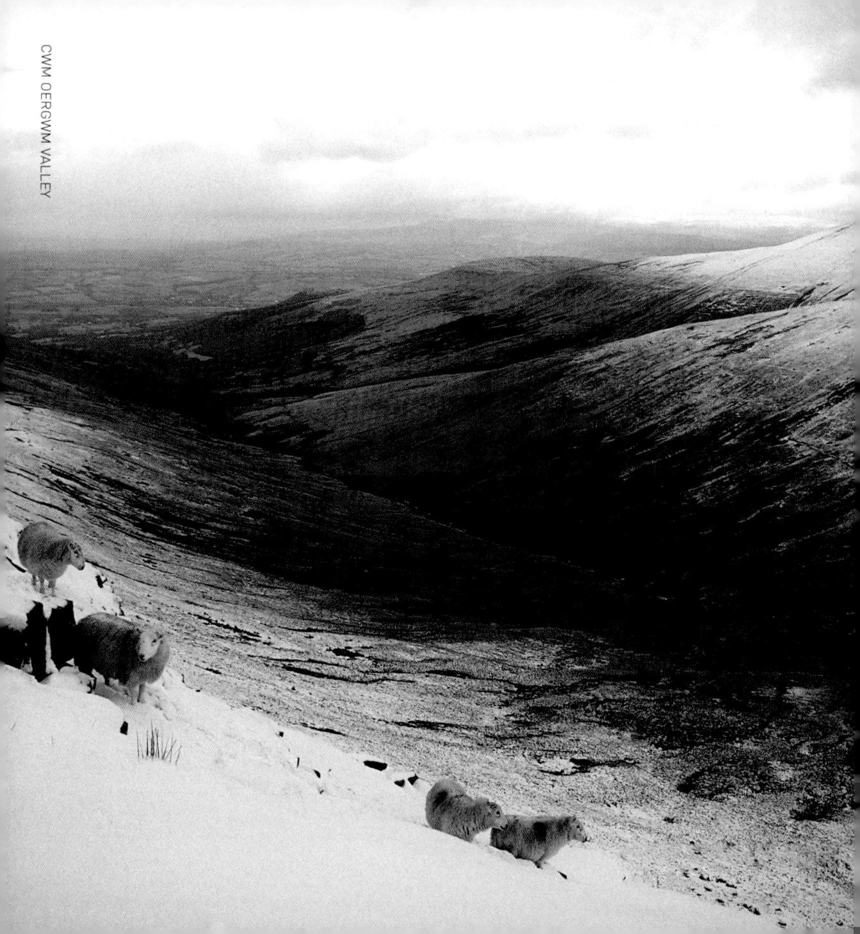

CWM OERGWM VALLEY

Harbourmaster Hotel
Aberaeron, SA46 0BA
Tel: 01545 570755
www.harbour-master.com
The restaurant at this hotel prides itself on its use of local produce, including Aberaeron prawns, Cardigan Bay crab and lobster, Aberaeron mackerel, Welsh Black beef and venison. Not open to non-residents on Sundays or Mondays.

Kilvert's Hotel
The Bull Ring, Hay-on-Wye, HR3 5AG
Tel: 01497 821042
The ivy-clad Georgian free house is popular with locals and tourists alike, with a small flagged outdoor terrace area in the front, a rustic oak-beamed bar serving real ales such as Brains Reverend James, along with bar meals like braised Welsh lamb, pizzas and pastas. The elegant restaurant specialises in lamb and fish dishes.

Kings Head Inn
1 Market Square, Llandovery,
SA20 0AB
Tel: 01550 720393
A comfortable 16th-century former coaching inn and drovers' bank set in the centre of town. The exposed stone walls, wood beams and open fires combine to give the inn a warm and convivial atmosphere. The excellent food is based on fresh and wholesome Welsh produce.

Royal Oak
Rhandirmwyn, Llandovery, SA20 0NY
Tel: 01550 760201
A proper old fashioned country pub overlooking the Tywi Valley and mountains. Stone and tile floors and an open fire give the bar a rustic atmosphere, while the restaurant is decorated in cottage style. In summer there's a pleasant garden for alfresco dining. Meals include venison casserole, Welsh black beef and chicken curry.

Pembrokeshire

INTRODUCTION

In Welsh Pen-Fro means
land's end and, fittingly,
Pembrokeshire's sinuous
coastline reaches out into
the waves of the Atlantic
Ocean like a gnarled fist.
Volcanic eruptions and
earth movements have left
a tortured rocky coastline
of some 160 miles (260km),
whose beauty and drama have
been recognised by National
Park status. In Pembrokeshire
you can take it easy on the
sandy beaches, make sport
out of those Atlantic waves, or
discover the mysteries of
St David's or the ancient
Preseli Hills.

NEWGALE BEACH

Unmissable attractions

Explore Milford Haven, described by Admiral Lord Nelson to be one of the world's finest harbours...walk across the Preseli Hills and look out for the famous blue dolomite stones that were transported from here to Wiltshire to build Stonehenge or seek out Pentre Ifan, Britain's largest and best preserved burial chambers...explore St David's, Britain's smallest city...enjoy fantastic walking and birding around the Marloes Peninsula...or take a ferry trip to Skomer's Island from Martin's Haven and relish the views of puffins, dolphins and, possibly, basking sharks...experience Fishguard's Music Festival in June or Tenby's Arts Festival in September...discover Solva, one of Pembrokeshire's most picturesque and popular resorts.

1

1 Pembroke
Magnificent Pembroke Castle occupies a commanding position between two tidal inlets.

2 Tenby
Boats trips from Tenby harbour offer the chance to see grey seals.

3 Marloes Sands
This spectacular beach, in sight of Skomer and Skokholm Islands, is cared for by the National Trust.

179

4 Milford Haven
The attractive Milford Haven estuary proves a safe and busy anchorage for all types of leisure craft.

5 Newport
The remarkable Newport Transport Bridge, which links the banks of the River Usk, was opened in 1906.

5

HAVERFORDWEST & ST BRIDES BAY

Sited on the Western Cleddau, one of the two wide rivers that flow into the Milford Haven, Haverfordwest was, before the arrival of the railways came, a thriving port with barges, small steamships and coasting vessels regularly docking on the quayside. The castle, built by the first Earl of Pembroke, Gilbert de Clare in the 12th century, dominates the village from a lofty crag above the river. As a Norman stronghold, Haverfordwest was attacked and burned to the ground by Llewelyn the Great, but the castle survived, as it did when besieged in 1405 by another Prince of Wales, Owain Glyn Dwr. However, Oliver Cromwell ordered its destruction following the Civil War. The substantial walls and keep are still an impressive sight.

Today Haverfordwest is a thriving market town, the principle shopping centre for the area. Many shops and cafés line the quayside. The town museum is housed in the castle off Church Street. Also worth seeing are the recently excavated ruins of the Augustinian Priory of St Mary and St Thomas the Martyr, a short walk from the town centre.

This is an excellent base from which to explore Pembrokeshire's West Coast and St Brides Bay. Facing west to the Atlantic, most of the St Brides beaches are exposed to the prevailing winds. This whips up the surf and makes them extremely popular for sports such as surfing, windsurfing and kite-surfing. The most northerly of these is Newgale Sands, where a golden sandy beach stretches 2 miles (3km) from Newgale village in the north to the rocks of Rickets Head. A tall shingle bank separates the beach from the village. Patrolling lifeguards designate the safe swimming areas.

There's another long sandy beach at Broadhaven, a lively resort with a good range of facilities. It's worth exploring the northern end to see natural rock arches and stacks. To the south lies Little Haven. This

183

Visit

SKOMER

There's also a summer ferry (not Mondays) to Skomer Island from Martin's Haven on the headland west of Marloes. On the short voyage you may be lucky enough to see porpoises and dolphins, or even a basking shark. You'll almost certainly see some of the 6,000 breeding pairs of puffins peeping from their burrows. Like much of the mainland Skomer Island is grit with dark volcanic cliffs, which accommodate southern Britain's largest colony of nesting seabirds. On the pink thrift and sea campion-decked clifftops are the remnants of an Iron Age civilisation – a standing stone, burial cairns, ancient field boundaries and the earthworks of hut circles. A number of footpaths criss-cross the island. Do not stray off the paths.

pretty village with a slipway, used by the lifeboat, and beach, is a popular place with sea anglers.

Most spectacular is Marloes Sands where exceptionally violent earth movements thrust up the rock strata to form steeply angled rocky cliffs that resemble the yacht sails caught in a great gust of wind. Marloes village is a 0.6-mile (1km) walk from the isolated sandy beach.

MILFORD HAVEN

'It's one of the world's finest harbours,' Admiral Lord Nelson claimed as he gazed admiringly across the vast blue waters of Milford Haven. And this lovely sheltered estuary has provided one of Britain's most important maritime strongholds since the days of the Tudor kings. And yet Milford Haven the town is a more recent affair, built and planned in the late 18th century by Sir William Hamilton, the husband of Nelson's mistress, Emma. In the 1960s the big ships arrived – carrying crude oil for processing in new refineries. Of these, only the Texaco plant now survives. Today Milford boasts a pleasant harbour front and marina, overlooked by the Georgian buildings of Hamilton Terrace. In 1991 memories were rekindled when the Tall Ships Race came to town.

NEWPORT

While its neighbour Fishguard is bustling with traffic rushing to make the ferry to Ireland on time, life in little Newport, tucked away in the far northwest corner of Pembrokeshire, chugs along at a more relaxed pace. Here the distinctive crag-topped Carn Ingli ('Angel Mountain') rises from the back gardens of the villagers' cottages, while small boats bobble from their moorings or lean against the sandbars of the Nevern Estuary. Although only 1,138-feet (347m) high Carn Ingli is distinctively rugged and its cloak of heather and gorse is capped by jagged outcrops of dolerite. The ramparts that remain from an Iron Age fort ring the summit of the hill, which is scattered with the foundations of those early settlers' circular huts.

Newport Castle is part fortress, part manor house – it has been

Visit

BURIAL CROMLECH

Pentre Ifan is probably the finest example of a neolithic burial cromlech in Wales. It dates back to around 3500 BC and its huge capstone measures over 16 feet (5m) long poised on three 8-foot (2.5m) uprights, which frame and capture Carn Ingli's mystical outlines to perfection, especially when the sun is low. The cromlech can be accessed free of charge and is well signposted from the A487 east of Newport and the B4329 Preseli road at Brynberian.

inhabited as a private dwelling for the past 150 years. Built in the 13th century by Norman baron William Fitzmartin, the castle was held for centuries by the powerful lords of Cemaes. As can be seen from its ruined battlements, the fortress was often involved in conflict, first in 1215 when captured and sacked by Llewelyn the Great, Prince of Wales, then by Owain Glyn Dwr. Fitzmartin also established St Mary's Church,

whose Norman square tower vies for dominance with the castle.

The River Nevern divides Newport's two beaches. On the north side there's an excellent sandy beach with safe bathing away from the currents of the river mouth. Parrog beach on the south side is for walkers who can stroll along the clifftops, past thickets of colourful gorse and shimmering sea pinks.

PEMBROKE

Pembroke is an attractive walled town with a 900-year history dating back to its Norman castle, which overlooks the town from its perch on a limestone crag. Surrounded by water on three sides, the castle, built by the Earls of Pembroke, was one of the biggest in Wales. The walls of the keep are 7 feet (2m) thick and 75 feet (23m) high. A secret underground passage burrows beneath the Great Hall to the harbour. Harry Tudor, the grandson of John of Gaunt and a descendant of Llewelyn the Great, was born in the castle. On returning

Visit

THE GUN TOWER MUSEUM

Built in 1851 to protect the Royal Naval Dockyard at Pembroke, the Gun Tower, which juts out into the wide waterway, now houses a museum illustrating Pembroke's military heritage. You can learn about life as experienced by one of Queen Victoria's soldiers who waited for an invasion that never came, see superb models of the old navy dockyard where more than 200 ships were built, and learn about the World War II flying boats – Pembroke was the world's largest flying boat base.

from exile he advanced with an army, defeated Richard III at Bosworth Field, and was crowned Henry VII.

Pembroke was designated an Outstanding Conservation Area in 1977. In the bustling main street, lined with both Georgian and Tudor buildings there are some fascinating shops, cafés and restaurants. A stroll by the river and Mill Pond will take you around the castle walls.

PRESELI HILLS

The Preseli Hills rise from Cardigan Bay at Fishguard and Newport and reach their highest point at Foel Cwmcerwyn some 1,760 feet (536m) above sea level. They're not that high by Welsh standards but these peaks have always been synonymous with all things spiritual. Preseli has sunsets that light up the whole of Cardigan Bay with a fiery glow, framed by the jagged silhouettes of strangely weathered summit tors.

Buried beneath your feet are the settlers from pre-history: the neolithic tribes who were here before the 'true Welsh', the Celts, came from across the sea. Cromlechs, the earthwork and stone remains of fortress walls and hut circles are liberally scattered across the map for you to discover. Stonehenge in Wiltshire was built from rocks hewn from the Preselis. The rock that the monoliths were carved from, an igneous spotted dolerite, is exclusive to Carnmenyn on the eastern side of the range.

When the Normans attacked Pembrokeshire they built a line of castles from Pembroke to Roch near St Davids. The Welsh were driven into the foothills of the Preseli and an imaginary line, the Landsker, was to divide the different tongues. If you've first visited the county's English-speaking south coast you may be surprised when you arrive at Rosebush, a tiny village that lies to the south of Foel Cwmcerwyn, for this friendly place is Welsh-speaking. The little village, which is the starting point for the best Preseli walks, has a campsite and one of the best inns in Wales, Tafarn y Sinc.

ST DAVID'S

Set on a windswept plateau, St David's, Britain's smallest city, is as isolated from urban life as it is possible to be. Flanked on either side by jagged dolerite crests of Carn Llidi and Carnedd-lleithr, this looks and feels as if it is an inhospitable corner of the world. And so it was when Dewi, a 6th-century Celtic

PRESELI HILLS

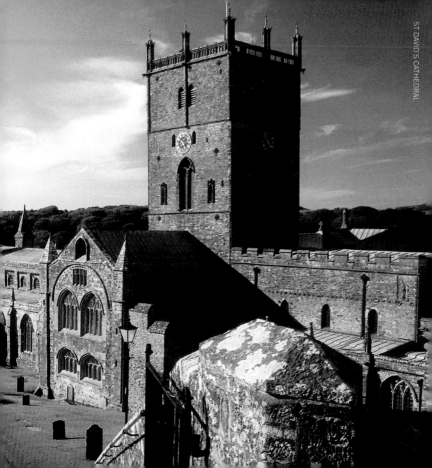

PEMBROKESHIRE

Activity

RAMSEY ISLAND

You can take the regular Ramsay Island boat from the slipway at St Justinian's, just 3 miles (5km) west of St David's and you will be transported across the fast-flowing Sound and infamous reef known as the Bitches to a haven for wildlife. Ramsey Island's rugged coastline, with its 300-foot (91m) cliffs and isolated rock coves, is home to the largest colony of grey seals in southwest Britain. Two small hills provide exhilarating walks with panoramas of Pembrokeshire's coast and islands through to the distant Preseli Hills.

hidden in the hollow of the Alun Valley behind Cross Square, and it's only when you descend down the Pebbles to the Bell Tower that they appear. At first glance the cathedral is as austere as the surrounding landscape, yet the purple-hued sandstone and perfect proportions give it an impressive presence. Inside, the cathedral is light and airy, with fine ornamental Norman arches and slightly leaning piers of the nave leading the eye to a impressive roof constructed of Irish oak.

Destroyed several times by the violent Viking raids in pre-Norman days, the oldest part of the current cathedral, the nave, dates back to 1180 – the original tower collapsed in 1220. In the early 14th century Bishop Henry de Gower raised the walls of the aisles, inserted much grander windows and built the south porch, transept chapels and Lady Chapel. A century later Bishop Vaughan built up the tower to its present height and added the splendid roof.

preacher who was later to become St David, patron saint of Wales, sailed from Ireland to set up his monastery here.

When you arrive in St David's and walk up the High Street past the gift shops, cottages, the boat-trip vendors' offices and the cafés, there are no signs of the grand ecclesiastical buildings. They're

The Reformation left the cathedral neglected and it was badly damaged during the Civil War. In 1862 George Gilbert Scott was charged with renovating it. While doing so he discovered two skeletons, believed to be St David and his friend St Justinian, now kept in an oak chest in the Holy Trinity Chapel. For around nine days in May and June each year, St David's Cathedral holds a festival of classical music. St David's Cathedral three cathedral choirs attend, as well as many top musicians from around the world.

Across the Alun stream lie the large and magnificent ruins of the Bishop's Palace. The palace was built in the late 12th century, but significantly enlarged by Bishop Henry de Gower between 1328 and 1347 to accommodate the growing number of pilgrims who flocked to St David's each year. St David's became a seat of power, illustrated by the opulent arcaded parapets and the magnificence of the Great Hall.

Today the palace is often a venue for concerts and plays. There are two permanent exhibitions: the Lords of the Palace and Life in the Palace of a Prince of the Church.

SAUNDERSFOOT

Once a small fishing village, which flourished with finds of high quality anthracite coal, Saundersfoot has since been caught up in near neighbour Tenby's popularity with visitors and holiday-makers. It's not hard to see why. Set at the foot of a pleasant wooded valley, the village has an attractive harbour alongside wonderful golden sands. The village is a popular centre for fishing, sailing and water sports.

SOLVA

Three miles (5km) east of St David's lies Solva, a village of two parts. The more modern upper village lines the A487 coast road, while in the lower, more attractive part, cottages, small shops and restaurants cluster around the harbour at the sheltered head of a long, winding tidal inlet. These days Solva is a busy little tourist trap but it was founded on maritime traditions. A thriving port until the arrival of the railways, it had several warehouses and a dozen or so limekilns. Solva once boasted a passenger service to New York. However, rather unusually, the passengers would have to bring their own food for a voyage that could last for up to four months!

Though it's a fine place for pottering about and having a spot of lunch, Solva is one of the best bases for a coastal walk, maybe to St David's (get the bus back), or just a stroll along the Gribbin, where there's an Iron Age settlement and a perfect view back to the village.

STACKPOLE

The 2,000-acre (810ha) estate, once owned by the powerful Scottish Cawdor family but now managed by the National Trust, is situated between Bosherton, Stackpole and St Govan's Head. It encompasses some of Pembrokeshire's finest coastal scenery.

Bosherton, a tiny village at the western end of the estate, is well situated for a visit to the Bosherton Lily Ponds. These were created by flooding three wooded limestone valleys. It has been claimed that this was the home of the Lady of the Lake and from where King Arthur gained his magical sword, Excalibur. It's certainly a magical place for nature lovers, who can wander through the surrounding woodland at the waters' edge to reach the seashore at Broad Haven beach. A June visit will reveal water lilies in full splendour, covering the waters of the Western Arm. Visitors include the cormorant, grey heron, kingfisher, coot and moorhen, and you're likely to see one of the many dragonfly, darting across the lakes.

There's another National Trust car park (toll) at Stackpole Quay near to the site of Stackpole Court. The mansion was demolished in 1963 when punitive taxes made

it necessary for the Cawdors to dispose of their Welsh assets. The quay, a tiny inlet with a stone-built harbour pier, marks a clearly visible transition between the old red sandstone cliffs of Manorbier and the limestone of southwest Pembrokeshire. A short walk across fields and clifftops leads to some steps descending into Barafundle Bay, a delectable and traffic-free golden sandy beach ideal for swimming or a spot of sunbathing. Further sojourns through the pines and sycamores at the far end of the bay take you to the cliffs, arches and stacks of Stackpole Head. The views from here stretch to Caldy Island to the Gower Peninsula in the distance. Beyond, to the south, you may be able to make out the lofty landform of Lundy Island.

If you time your visit for when the military are not training, you can take the minor road leading south from Bosherton to St Govan's car park. Steps lead down to the 13th-century St Govan's Chapel, a

Visit

STACK ROCKS AND THE GREEN BRIDGE OF WALES

Probably the most photographed feature on the Pembrokeshire coast is the Green Bridge of Wales, a huge natural arch formed by the collapsing of two coastal caverns. It can be viewed from the platform on Stack Rocks, which are also known as Elegug Stacks. Before setting out on the road west of Castlemartin barracks, find out if the military are on exercise (Tel: 01646 662287).

tiny building wedged into a fissure at the base of the cliffs on the site of a Celtic hermit's cell. St Govan, an 11th-century saint, is believed to have been buried beneath the altar.

TENBY

Tenby, by far the biggest and most successful of Pembrokeshire's resorts, is surrounded by caravan sites and it's often buzzing with coach parties and holiday-makers

Activity

CALDEY ISLAND

A boat trip from Tenby to Caldey Island is like a journey back in time, with quiet tracks wending through fields of barley and footpaths seeking out secluded cliff-ringed coves. In 1929 Cistercian monks founded a monastery on Caldey. They farmed the island's 600 acres (240ha) and made perfume from the flowers and herbs. Walkers can seek out the ruins of the old priory or climb to lofty vantage points for stunning views of the coast.

with those cottages and the old castle floodlit against the night sky.

Tenby has two distinct parts. Within the largely intact medieval town walls many of its ancient narrow streets have been cobbled to re-create their authenticity, but outside of these walls, overlooking the large South Beach, the Victorian's influence is there for all to see, with traditional terraces.

Castle Hill looks down on the old and new towns, but little remained of the castle after its destruction in the Civil War. Much of the town's history from the Stone Age to present times can be traced by visiting the Tenby Museum and Art Gallery on Castle Hill. This includes charters and privileges granted by the Tudors and the Earls of Pembroke.

A devised town trail visits the walls and many of the historic buildings, including the Tudor Merchant's House (National Trust), which is fitted out with authentic furnishings and has three walls with the remains of early frescoes.

from all backgrounds. On Bank Holidays the town feels like it's going to burst with the weight of its own popularity. But Tenby has undeniable beauty. Brightly colour-washed cottages wrap themselves around a small sandy beach, framed by the pier of the lifeboat station, the harbour and the small boats in the bay. When the coach parties have gone home you can take an after-dinner stroll along the promenade

TOURIST INFORMATION CENTRES

Haverfordwest
19 Old Bridge Street.
Tel: 01437 763110

Milford Haven
94 Charles Street.
Tel: 01646 690866

Newport
2 Bank Cottages, Long Street.
Tel: 01239 820912

Pembroke
Commons Road. Tel: 01646 622388

St David's
National Park Visitor Centre,
The Grove. Tel: 01437 720392

Saundersfoot
Harbour Car Park.
Tel: 01834 813672

Tenby
The Croft. Tel: 01834 842404

PLACES OF INTEREST

Caldey Island
Off Tenby. Tel: 01834 844453;
www.caldey-island.co.uk
Take a boat trip from Tenby.
Benedictine monastery, quiet walks,
and fine beaches.

Castell Henllys
Off the A487 between Newport
(Pembrokeshire) and Cardigan.
Tel: 01239 891319;
www.castellhenllys.com

Dinosaur Park
Gumfreston, Tenby.
Tel: 01834 45272;
www.thedinosaurpark.co.uk
A 1-mile (1.6km) long walk with
dinosaurs and woodland trail.

Folly Farm
Begelly, Kilgetty.
Tel: 01834 812731
A family adventure park with a fun
fair, theatre, play barn, exotic animals,
restaurant and coffee shop.

The Gun Tower Museum
Pembroke Dock.
Tel: 01646 622246
Pembrokeshire's naval heritage.

Pembroke Castle
Tel: 01646 684585;
www.pembrokecastle.co.uk

St David's Bishop's Palace
Tel: 01437 720517
Extensive ruins next to cathedral.

St David's Cathedral
www.stdavidscathedral.org.uk
Tenby Museum and Art Gallery
Castle Hill, Tenby.
Tel: 01834 842809

FOR CHILDREN
Oakwood Theme Park
Narberth. Roller coasters and more.
Tel: 01834 891376;
www.oakwoodthemepark.co.uk
Teifi Valley Narrow Gauge Railway
Nr Newcastle Emlyn.
Tel: 01559 371077;
www.teifivalleyrailway.co.uk

SHOPPING
Market Days
Fishguard, Thu; farmers market
fortnightly, Sat.
Haverfordwest, fortnightly.
Pembroke Dock, Fri;
St David's, WI market, Thu.
Tenby, indoor market, Mon, Tue,
Thu–Sat.
Narberth
Antiques shops.

PERFORMING ARTS
Fishguard
Theatr Gwaun.
Milford Haven
Torch Theatre.
Narberth
Queens Hall.

SPORTS & ACTIVITIES
ANGLING
Coastal Fishing
Amroth for bass, flounder and
mackerel (boat hire); Haken Point,
Milford Haven for dogfish, bass, and
pollack; Whitesand Bay for bass and
flatfish.
Coarse Fishing
Peterstone Coarse Lakes, Wentloog,
Newport for huge carp, bream and
tench.
Tel: 01633 680905
Yet-y-Gors Fishery, Manorowen,
Fishguard. Tel: 01348 873497;
www.yet-y-gors.co.uk
Lakes for carp bream, roach, rudd,
perch and tench. Fly fishing for trout
also available.

River Fishing

The Nevern, which rises from the Preseli Hills and flows out to sea at Newport, is very good for sea trout.

BEACHES

Barafundel Bay

Popular with sun seekers, walkers and swimmers. Accessed from the Stackpole Quay car park.

Broadhaven, St Brides Bay

Another long sandy beach popular for watersports.

Dale

A shingle beach well known for yachting, diving and windsurfing.

Freshwater West

Big Atlantic waves make this sand and shingle beach ideal for surfers.

Little Haven, St Brides Bay

Small sheltered cove next to the village.

Manorbier

Popular with surfers.

Marloes Sands

Crescent shaped sandy beach with rock outcrops.

Newgale Sands, St Brides Bay

Exposed beach popular for surfing and kite surfing.

Saundersfoot

Popular sandy beach beyond the harbour.

Tenby North

The little sandy beach is overlooked by the harbour and town's old quarters.

Tenby South

A good expanse of sand, popular with bathers.

Whitesands, St David's

Fine long sandy beach with safe swimming and surfing areas designated by the summer lifeguards.

BOAT TRIPS

Tenby Harbour to Caldey Island

Tel: 01834 844453

Brunel Quay, Neyland to Grassholm, Skokholm and Skomer

Dale Sailing.
Tel: 01646 603124;
www. dale-sailing.co.uk

St Justinian to Ramsey Island
Several companies operate boat trips from St Justinian near St David's to Ramsey Island.
Booking offices in St David's.
Useful websites:
www.ramseyisland.co.uk
www.thousandislands.co.uk

CYCLING
Llys-y-fran
An 8-mile (12.8km) circuit of the reservoir 8 miles (12.8km) northeast of Haverfordwest.
Neyland to Johnston railway path
The path is 5 miles (8km) each way.

HORSE-RIDING
Dunes Riding Centre
Cotts Lane, Martlewy, Narberth.
Tel: 01834 891398

East Nolton Riding Stables
East Nolton Farm, Nolton Haven, Haverfordwest. Tel: 01437 710360

Havard Stables
Trewiddyg Fawr, Dinas Cross, Newport.
Tel: 01348 811452

Llanwnda Riding & Trecking
Penrhiw Fach, Llanwnda, Goodwick.
Tel: 01348 873595

WALKING
Pembrokeshire Coast Path
A good bus service for walkers operates along the whole length of the path. Pembrokeshire Coastal Bus
Tel: 01437 776313;
www.pembrokeshiregreenways.co.uk

ANNUAL EVENTS & CUSTOMS
Fishguard
Fishguard Folk Festival, May.
Fishguard International Music Festival, Jun.
Fishguard Jazz Festival, Sep.
Narberth
Winter Carnival, Dec.
St David's
Cathedral Festival, May/Jun.
Tenby
Arts Festival, late Sep.

TEA ROOMS

The Boathouse Tea Room
Stable Yard, Stackpole, SA71 5DE
Tel: 01646 672058
Close to the old stone jetty, this popular licensed café has a large outdoor area for alfresco dining. The quiches are delicious while tasty sandwiches include fresh crab, and cream teas have tempting cakes.

Morawelon Café Bar & Restaurant
Parrog, Newport, SA42 0RW
Tel: 01239 820565
Set on the Parrog beachfront, you can indulge yourself here with many varieties of tea or coffee and delicious cakes, or you can tuck into a mouth-watering meal that might include freshly caught local crab, washed down with a cool glass of white wine.

The Old Printing House
20 Main Street, Solva, SA62 6UU
Tel: 01437 721603
The award-winning tea room/restaurant is located at the heart of the village in an 18th-century house and paper mill with beamed ceilings and stripped stone walls. The tea room is noted for its freshly baked bread and cakes, home-made chutneys and cream teas.

Tudor Lodge Restaurant
Jameston, Manorbier, SA70 7SS
Tel: 01834 871978
www.tudorlodgerestaurant.co.uk
This restaurant has a clean, modern style with walls hung with contemporary paintings and a good atmosphere, but with traditional, blazing log fires for when the sun cools. The food is excellent and prepared using fresh local produce wherever possible, whether it is for light lunches or evening meals.

LOWER FISHGUARD

Cambrian Inn

6, Main Street, Solva
SA62 6UU
Tel: 01437 721210

The 17th-century inn sited at the entrance to Lower Solva offers both restaurant and bar meals in comfortable cosy surroundings. Expect to see fresh pasta dishes, steaks and vegetarian dishes with real ales such as Brains Reverend James. No children under 10 or dogs in the bar.

St Brides Inn

St Brides Road, Little Haven,
SA62 3UN
Tel: 01437 781266

This charming little inn has wooden pews inside a compact dining area, with stripped stone walls and an ancient well in one corner. Good food is served here with a daily specials board that often includes locally caught seafood. There's also a beer garden, where meals and barbecues are served throughout the summer.

The Stackpole Inn

Jasons Corner, Stackpole, SA71 5DF
Tel: 01646 672324
www.stackpoleinn.co.uk

The 17th-century Stackpole Inn is popular with walkers and locals. The extensive, award-winning bar and restaurant menu includes fresh locally caught fish that appear on the 'just in' specials board and old favourites such as Welsh black beef.

Tafarn Sinc

Rosebush, SA66 7QT
Tel: 01437 532214

The red-painted corrugated building that used to be a railway halt promises little on first sight, and when you realise that there's sawdust on the floor you might be put off. But this Welsh-speaking, friendly pub has been likened to a museum of local history inside, with old photos and curios on every wall. The pub has its own-brewed beer, Cwrw Tafarn Sinc, and serves delicious food including the most succulent steaks.

WORM'S HEAD

Gower Peninsula & Coast

INTRODUCTION

Though not far from the urban valleys of the south, the limestone cliffs and golden sandy bays of the Gower Peninsula have been protected from unsympathetic development – industrial and residential – since it was designated as Britain's first Area of Outstanding Natural Beauty in 1956. Further east, Cardiff is in every sense the capital of Wales. It has a rich industrial, commercial and cultural heritage, but has evolved into a modern, vibrant and cosmopolitan city. Cardiff's docks have become vibrant Cardiff Bay, fringed visitor attractions, restaurants, bars and shops.

NASH POINT

Unmissable attractions

Enjoy shopping, good food, an array of cultural treats and a host of other treats in Cardiff...explore historic Monmouth, the birthplace of Henry V...go in search of the poet, Dylan Thomas at Laugharne...explore the Gower Peninsula and discover superb Rhossili Bay and coast...discover two castles at Grosmont and Skenfrith on a quiet cycle ride.

1

2

1 Rhossili
Rhossili Bay is one of the finest stretches of flat sands in Wales and an excellent place for walking.

2 Cardiff
Cardiff's Millennium Stadium, in the heart of the city, hosts major sporting events and concerts.

HOT SPOTS

3

3 Port Einon Bay
One of the most popular bays on the Gower, Port Einon is popular with both families and surfers.

4 Monmouth
Little remains of Monmouth's early Norman castle, built on a hill above the River Monnow.

5 Parkmill
Remote Three Cliffs Beach takes its name from the three cliffs that project out into the bay. The beach can be accessed via a signposted path from Parkmill.

4

5

CARDIFF

Today the capital of Wales is the pride of the principality, a flourishing modern city, but one that hasn't forgotten its roots. Its history goes back 2,000 years to the time of the Romans and it's all encompassed within the walls of Cardiff Castle which stands proudly, right in the centre of the city. The moated Norman castle, whose 12th-century keep has survived, was built on the site of the Roman fort – some of the Roman foundation walls can still be seen. Like many Welsh castles, Cardiff was left ruinous by Owain Glyn Dwr but it was rebuilt by Richard Beauchamp, the Earl of Warwick, and continued to serve as a residence for several centuries.

Cardiff's prosperity, and gradual rise to importance, came with the Industrial Revolution. The discovery of coking coal allowed the iron-smelting industry to flourish in the valleys to the north and Cardiff became the obvious choice as a port. At this time the wealthy Bute family, who were descendants of the royal Stuarts, moved here. They enlarged the docks and made Cardiff into one of the world's largest coal and iron exporting ports, and they also took possession of Cardiff Castle. The 3rd Marquis of Bute commissioned William Burges to redevelop the living quarters into the Gothic Victorian style you see today. No expense was spared: the interiors were opulent, using marble, gold leaf and fine hardwoods from around the world. Many of the rooms have amazing decorated ceilings, stained-glass windows, murals of historical and mythological figures, and fine works of art on the walls. The ornate clock tower looks over the city, as Big Ben does in London.

The city centre buildings are a mix of modern, Victorian and Edwardian, with shopping arcades criss-crossing the main streets. The classic Portland stone buildings of the Law Courts, City Hall and the National Museum present an impressive front to the Civic Centre

CARDIFF

Visit

CASTELL COCH – THE RED CASTLE

This fairy-tale castle, a few miles north of Cardiff, echoes those in Bavaria with its circular red sandstone towers and conical roofs. Built on a limestone outcrop on wooded hill-slopes, the original Norman castle had fallen into disrepair, but the 3rd Marquis of Bute commissioned William Burges to refurbish it to the same extravagant standards that he exercised on Cardiff Castle.

and university areas, while the open spaces of Bute Park behind the castle take you to the banks of the River Taff. Here you can catch a waterbus past the famous Cardiff Arms Park and the much larger Millennium Stadium to Cardiff Bay, where the old dockyards, which declined with the end of the Welsh coalfield, have been transformed into a busy, thriving waterfront. The controversial Cardiff Bay Barrage construction has created a massive freshwater lake out of the bay, but still allows the fish to pass through.

On the attractive, vibrant waterfront the famous terracotta Pierhead Building is joined by two revolutionary new buildings: the Senedd Building, which houses the National Assembly of Wales, and the Millennium Centre, which presents the performing arts. The latter built from local slate has a bilingual inscription in large letters: 'In these stones horizons sing', which says a lot about 21st-century Cardiff.

LAUGHARNE & WEST CARMARTHEN COASTLINE

Lying on the western bank of the Taf, Laugharne, which is pronounced Larn, is dominated by the imposing shell of its Norman castle. The castle is perched on a tree-cloaked cliff looking out across the salt marshes and creeks of the estuary and was immortalised by J M W Turner. The main street, lined with Georgian houses, antiquarian shops and bistros, leads to the unusual

LAUGHARNE CASTLE

whitewashed town hall, which has a modest clock tower. Laugharne and Malmesbury in Wiltshire are the only two United Kingdom towns to have retained a charter granted by Royal Decree. The charter, kept in the town hall, allows the people to be governed by a corporation in addition to other tiers of government.

Laugharne is synonymous with Dylan Thomas, the Welsh poet and author of *Under Milk Wood*, who lived here off and on for many years. Thomas spent the last four years of his life (1949–53) at the Boathouse. This romantically situated cottage overlooking the estuary is now a museum dedicated to his life and works. Visitors can also view his writing shed, sited on a terrace above the house.

Moving out in Carmarthen Bay the road from Laugharne comes to Pendine, whose firm beach of sands and shells stretches for 7 miles (11km) between Gilman Point to Laugharne Sands. In the early 20th century the beach was considered ideal for world land speed records, including Malcolm Campbell's 146.16mph (235.22kmph) record in 1924. These ended with the fatal accident of Parry Thomas-Jones, whose car, Babs, rolled over in the 1927 attempt for the world land speed record. Babs can be seen in Pendine's Museum of Speed. Note: The beach is owned by the MoD and they do occasionally restrict public access in the area.

MONMOUTH & WYE VALLEY

Historic Monmouth stands at the confluence of the rivers Wye and Monnow. It was the birthplace of Henry V, whose statue stands in Agincourt Square looking down upon a statue of another of the town's favourite sons, Henry Rolls, aviation pioneer and co-founder of Rolls Royce. Monmouth's 13th-century bridge over the River Monnow is the only one in Britain to have included a fortified Gatehouse, which at one time would have had a portcullis and sentry rampart.

The town is a good base for an exploration of the picturesque Wye Valley and its lovely riverside walks. Just a few miles south lies Tintern Abbey, founded by the Cistercian order in the 12th century. Though roofless, the abbey's graceful arches of the Decorated style and great windows remain almost complete, embellished by their exquisite surroundings in the wooded and tranquil Wye valley.

Chepstow, near the mouth of the Wye, is known for its massive Norman castle, which stands on formidable cliffs high above the river. It's best viewed from the east bank.

PARKMILL

Parkmill shelters in the shady sylvan bowers of Ilston Cwm, a limestone valley that winds its way from inland Gower to the coast at Threecliff Bay. Centred around the only working mill on the peninsula the village is popular with both tourists who come to see the Gower Heritage Centre, with its craft workshops

Visit

KIDWELLY CASTLE

Built on a steep grassy mound looking down on the River Gwendraeth, Kidwelly is one of the best-preserved castles in South Wales. The old timber castle built by the Normans in the early 12th century was destroyed in a heavy attack by Llewellyn the Great in 1231, but was rebuilt in the 1270s. Unusually, the superb gatehouse forms part of the outer walls. It is now managed by CADW.

and museum, and walkers. To the northwest you can take a stroll through the woods of Green Cwm to visit the Giant's Grave, a megalithic tomb dating back to 3500 BC, or head southwards down Ilston Cwm. This route leads through more woodland before continuing beneath the huge dunes of Pennard Burrows, on top of which lie the ruins of Pennard Castle and its neighbouring church. The 13th-century castle, which was built by the Normans, appears in few

Visit

OXWICH NATIONAL NATURE RESERVE

As an area of Outstanding Natural Beauty, Oxwich Bay combines wildlife with all the appeal of a superb beach resort. It is an excellent location for swimming, surfing and nature appreciation. The beach is easily accessible and the reserve supports several diverse wildlife habitats, including freshwater lakes and marshes, swamps, salt marshes, dunes, cliffs and woodland. The freshwater marsh was artificially created when Sir Thomas Mansel Talbot of Penrice Estate built a wall to prevent encroachment from the sea. The reserve has more than 600 species of flowering plants. You are likely to see ringed plovers, curlews, oystercatchers and gulls feeding on the wet sands at low tide, along with wigeons and warblers on the marshes.

historical records and has always been dogged by sand encroachment. To this day, known remnants remain buried deep in the sands for their own preservation.

The now lazy stream meanders and trickles into the beautiful golden sands of Threecliff Bay beneath the stunning, almost vertical limestone strata of the Three Cliffs. The popular climbers' crags begin a fine stretch of superb cliff scenery past the houses of Southgate to Pwlldu Head. Pwlldu means Blackpool, but that's where the similarity ends, for you'll find yourself looking down from this massive headland to a pebble storm beach at the head of the lovely wooded limestone gorge of the Bishopston Valley.

Surfers love the commercialised Caswell Bay, a lovely sandy cove overlooked by pines and self-catering holiday apartments and great waves for their sport. At Mumbles the world of Gower has collided with that of urban Swansea. A pier, amusement parlours, ice cream kiosks and cafés make country lovers feel they want to retreat rather quickly back to real Gower, although the children may wish to stay, play and eat.

CASWELL BAY

TO THE GLORY OF GOD
AND IN MEMORY OF
WILLIAM (BILLY) GIBBS, COXSWAIN
WILLIAM EYNON, SECOND COXSWAIN
GEORGE HARRY, LIFEBOATMAN
WHO WERE DROWNED OFF PORT EINON
ON 1ST JANUARY 1916 WHEN THE PORT EINON
LIFEBOAT "JANET" TWICE CAPSIZED IN THE
ENDEAVOUR TO RENDER

PORT EINON

After threading through the outskirts of Swansea, the wide-open spaces of Fairwood Common, and flirting with the coast at Pennard, Gower's only major road, the A4118 ends at little Port Einon on the southwest coast. The last stretch through the village is narrow, rarely wide enough for two cars to pass. The village is a mix of Gower's rugged coastline and small-scale commercialism. Dunes and cobbles line a sandy beach, all then surrounded by rugged cliffs dotted with the typical Gower lime-washed cottages. There's a real old-fashioned seaside atmosphere, with beachwear, and bucket and spade shops, a couple of fish and chip shop cafés and a surf shop. However, the a short walk away is the rugged cliffs and secluded rocky coves. The coastal walk to Worms Head and Rhossili is the finest in Gower.

Port Einon gets its name from the 11th-century Welsh prince, Einon ap Owain and it is believed that he built the long-gone Port Einon.

The village's history is inextricably linked to the sea. In its heyday of the 19th-century more than 40 oyster skiffs operated from the port, and limestone from a nearby quarry was exported. The blue-green stones you'll see scattered on the shoreline are not part of Gower geology but ballast from the cargo ships.

Tales of smuggling are common and it is said that the old salt house, the ruin beneath the cliffs of the western promontory, was used by the Lucas family as a storehouse for contraband. At one time there were eight customs and excise officers based here. Next to the salt house is the youth hostel. The building was formerly a lifeboat station but this was closed following a rescue attempt that went dreadfully wrong. Called out during a winter storm of 1916 the volunteer crew were caught out by horrendous waves, which capsized the boat twice, drowning three of the crew. A monument has been erected in the churchyard as a tribute to their bravery.

RHOSSILI BEACH

Oxwich Point separates Port Einon Bay from the larger sandy sweep of Oxwich Bay, an ideal location for swimming and surfing and also appealing to nature lovers who can visit the nature reserve. The ruins of Sir Rice Mansel's magnificent Tudor mansion, known as Oxwich Castle are perched on the headland overlooking the bay. It is now managed by CADW.

RHOSSILI

At the western end of the peninsula facing Carmarthen Bay, Rhossili is the pride of Gower: a perfect, gently arcing sandy beach flanked by the 250-foot (76m) sandstone cliffs and steep grassy flanks of Rhossili Down. It owes much its wild nature to the steep-sided down that presides over its relentless waves and provides a natural and impenetrable barrier to development. The down is a 633-feet (193m) high, whaleback ridge that runs almost the full length of the beach. The path that traces the ridge

Visit

THE GOWER HERITAGE CENTRE

Themed around a 12th-century water-powered corn mill built by the Norman baron, William de Breos, the Gower Heritage Centre opened in 1990 as a countryside crafts centre. Visitors can explore the sawmill, wheelwright's shop, miller's cottage, agricultural museum, craft shop and tea room. There's a children's play area and numerous small animals and recently housed exhibits from the former Maritime Museum in Swansea.

Activity

THE WORMS HEAD

The string of islets that thrust defiantly into the Atlantic at the bay's southernmost tip is known as Worms Head. It is now a nature reserve, but can be reached at low tide by scrambling across the rocky causeway at the western tip of the promontory. It's essential that you check the tide timetables before making such a sortie, as it's easy to be cut off by the surprising tenacity of the rising tides.

is one of the fairest places to walk in the whole of South Wales.

Each day high tide makes islands out of the tiny outcrop of Burry Holms in the north and the one-mile (1.6km) long rocky spit of Worms Head in the south. On many days the breeze is up and the bay is full of surfers riding the waves. When the tide is out you'll see the wooden skeleton of the coaster, Helvetia, driven ashore by the gales of 1887. Rhossili Down at 632 feet (193m) is the highest place on Gower; there's a splendid bridleway straddling its heights. On the summit are the Sweyne's Howes burial chambers.

Rhossili village has one large hotel, a National Trust information centre and shop. A car park gives access to the beach and Worms Head. Tides are of the utmost importance for those wanting to scramble across the rocky causeway to the headland: consult the timetables posted on the NT shop and the coastguard's station.

SWANSEA

Little is recorded of Swansea until the Norman conquerors saw its potential as a port. In 1106 Henry de Beaumont, 1st earl of Warwick, built a castle on a cliff overlooking the mouth of the Tawe. After the Welsh sacked the castle in the 13th century, it was rebuilt. The current building dates back to the 14th century, though it didn't have much of a strategic role following the defeat of the Welsh by Edward I. In 1306 Swansea was given the Royal Charter to build and repair ships.

During the 19th century large-scale anthracite mining and the metal industry changed this small village into the metropolis it is today. By the 1850s the railways had arrived, the first dockyard had been completed and Swansea was supplying 60 per cent of the world's copper. Swansea's other face was of that of a seaside resort – railway adverts compared Swansea Bay with the Bay of Naples and well-to-do Victorians came to take the sea air.

SWANSEA MARINA

World War II bombing and the mid-20th-century decline in manufacturing saw the city having to re-invent itself. Still a little down-at-heel in the suburbs, Swansea has become a vibrant city, full of culture and new ideas. The dock area has been redeveloped into an opulent Maritime Quarter, where refurbished old buildings share streets with modern architecture such as the National Waterfront Museum, and where you can see vivid reminders of the city's industrial and maritime past. Take a stroll around the 600-berth yachting marina and over the elegant Sail Bridge across the Tawe, then pop in to see the exhibition at the Dylan Thomas Centre.

A fine shopping centre surrounds the castle. Music lovers can see international artists at Brangwyn Hall or operas at the Grand Theatre. The Glynn Vivian Art Gallery, which has a fine collection of paintings and sculpture from old masters and modern artists, also has displays of Swansea porcelain.

GOWER PENINSULA & COAST

TOURIST INFORMATION CENTRES
Caerleon
5 High Street.
Tel: 01633 422656
Cardiff Visitor Centre
The Old Library, The Hayes.
Tel: 02920 227281
Chepstow
Castle Car Park, Bridge Street.
Tel: 01291 623772
Monmouth
Shire Hall, Agincourt Square.
Tel: 01600 713899
Swansea
Plymouth Street. Tel: 01792 468321

PLACES OF INTEREST
The Big Pit: National Coal Museum
Blaenavon.
Tel: 01496 790311;
www.museumwales.ac.uk/en/bigpit
The Boat House
Dylan's Walk, Laugharne
Tel: 01994 427420;
www.dylanthomasboathouse.com
Caerleon
Newport.
www.caerleon.net

Caerphilly Castle
Tel: 029 2088 3143;
www.caerphillycastle.com
Cardiff Castle
Castle Street, Cardiff.
Tel: 029 2087 8100;
www.cardiffcastle.com
Castell Coch
Castle Street, Cardiff.
Tel: 029 20878100/20810101
Dylan Thomas Centre
Somerset Place, Swansea.
Tel: 01792 463980;
www.dylanthomas.org
Gower Heritage Centre
Parkmill, Gower.
Tel: 01792 371206;
www.gowerheritagecentre.co.uk
Laugharne Castle
Tel: 01994 427906
Llandaff Cathedral
Llanerch Vineyard
Hensol, Pendoylan, Vale of Glamorgan.
Tel: 01443 225877;
www.llanerch-vineyard.co.uk
Museum of Speed
Pendine. Tel: 01994 453488
Local land speed attempts and racing.

The National Botanic Garden of Wales
Llanarthne.
Tel: 01558 668768;
www.gardenofwales.org.uk

National Museum
Cathays Park, Cardiff.
Tel: 029 20397951;
www.museumwales.ac.uk/en/cardiff

National Waterfront Museum
Oystermouth Road, Swansea.
Tel: 01792 638950
Tells the story of the industrialisation
of Wales with exhibits, including
working engines.

Raglan Castle
Tel: 01291 690228
Off A40 between Monmouth and
Abergavenny.

Rhondda Heritage Park
Lewis Merthyr Colliery, Trehafod.
Tel: 01443 682036;
www.rhonddaheritagepark.com

Senedd Building
Pierhead Street, Cardiff Bay
Waterfront.

FOR CHILDREN
Pembrey Country Park
Burry Port.
Tel: 01554 833913 (Parks Manager).
Seaside park with crazy golf, dry ski
slope, toboggan run and a miniature
railway.

SHOPPING
Cardiff
Extensive shopping in a traffic-free
environment. Several Victorian arcades
full of small independent shops and
many of the larger chain stores.

Swansea
Extensive shopping opportunities in
and around the Quadrant Centre (an
indoor mall). There's a particularly
good indoor market selling delicious
fresh, local produce.

PERFORMING ARTS
Brangwyn Hall
Swansea. Tel: 01792 635489
Chapter Arts Centre
Cardiff. Tel: 029 2031 1050
Grand Theatre
Swansea. Tel: 01792 475715
Millennium Centre
Cardiff. Tel: 0870 402000
New Theatre
Monmouth.
Tel: 029 2087 8889
St David's Hall
Cardiff. Tel: 029 2087 8444
Savoy Theatre
Tel: 01600 750488

SPORTS & ACTIVITIES
BEACHES
Barry Island
Two excellent beaches for bathers.
Carmarthenshire
Cefn Sidan, Pembrey Sands.
Eight miles (13km) of fine sands and
dunes accessed from Pembrey Country
Park near Burry Port. Patrolled by
lifeguards in summer.

Caswell Bay
Excellent small beach, popular with
surfers. Good café. No dogs May–Sep.
Glamorgan Heritage Coast
Porthcawl.
The town's four beaches here are
popular for bathing and watersports.
Oxwich Bay
Sand dunes overlook Gower's sandy
beach, second largest. Good for
bathing, canoeing and sailing, also
surfing when the wind is up.
Pendine Sands
An 'endless' beach that once facilitated
land speed record attempts.
Port Einon Bay
Commercialised beach with cafés,
campsites and gift shops. No dogs
May–Sep.
Rhossili Bay
Huge crescent-shaped sandy cove,
popular with surfers and hang-gliders.
BOAT TRIPS
Mumbles to Gower Coast and Caldey
Island.
Gower Explorer
Tel: 07810 407007;
www.gowerexplorer.co.uk

Bay Island Voyages
Lock Keeper's Cottage, Britannia Park
Cardiff.
Cruises around Cardiff Bay and the
coast.
Tel: 01446 420692;
www.bayisland.co.uk

CYCLING

Swansea Bike Path
This former railway track between
Gowerton and Black Pill (Swansea Bay)
is now a cycle path.

Tawe Riverside Path
From Clydach/Glais in Swansea Valley
to city's maritime quarter.

CYCLE HIRE

Monmouth Cycle Hire
7, St Vincents Drive, Monmouth.
Tel: 07782 270114

Afan Valley
Glyncorrwg, Port Talbot.
Tel: 01639 893661

HORSE-RIDING

Llanthony Riding and Trekking
Court Farm, Llanthony.
Tel: 01873 890359;
www.llanthony.co.uk

Marros Riding Centre
Marros, Pendine.
Tel: 01994 453238;
www.marros-farm.co.uk

Parc-Le-Breos Riding Centre
Penmaen, Gower.
Tel: 01792 371636;
www.parc-le-breos.co.uk

WALKING

Long Distance Routes
The Gower Way runs from Penlle'r
Castell to Rhossili.

ANNUAL EVENTS & CUSTOMS

Cardiff
Summer Festival, Jul–Aug.

Chepstow
Agricultural Show, mid-Aug.

Monmouth
Monmouth Festival, end Jul.

National Eisteddfod of Wales
Choirs, concerts and exhibitions, Aug.

Swansea
Swansea Festival of Music and Arts,
Oct.
Celebration of arts and entertainment.

TEA ROOMS

Crema Coffee Shop
Millennium Centre, Cardiff, CF10 5AL
Tel: 02920 484884

This is a stylish modern venue in the buzzing heart of the arts centre serving mouth-watering cakes, including wicked chocolate fudge cake, with a wide range of coffees and teas.

Norwegian Church
Harbour Drive, Cardiff Bay,
Cardiff, CF10 4PA
Tel: 02920 2049 3331

Built in 1869 as a place of worship for the large number of Scandinavian sailors in Cardiff, the white wooden building has a popular tea room where you can indulge yourself with excellent cakes and a range of snacks.

Part y Seal
Grosmont, NP7 8LE
Tel: 01981 240814

Here you can enjoy a relaxing morning coffee, lunch or afternoon tea in a splendid rural setting. The old stone cottage has delightful gardens for alfresco summer dining or glowing fires for the short winter days. The produce is home grown and organic. There's also an Oriental giftware shop and Fairytaleland with its seasonally changing scenes.

Café at the National Waterfront Museum
Oystermouth Road, Maritime Quarter,
Swansea SA1 3RD.
Tel: 01792 638950

Situated at the heart of the ultra-modern museum buildings in Swansea's Maritime Quarter, the café offers a good choice of excellent cakes, sandwiches, quiches, various savouries and appetising hot meals. Everything is made on the site using fresh produce sourced locally wherever possible. High chairs are available.

RHONDDA VALLEY

Abbey Hotel

Llanthony Priory, Llanthony, NP7 7NN
Tel: 01873 890487

Many pubs are next door to a church, but this one is in the grounds of the Cistercian priory. Serves lunches and evening meals (also ice creams and hot drinks). Refreshments under the cloisters – what a setting!

Bell at Skenfrith

Skenfrith, Monmouthshire, NP7 8UH
Tel: 01600 750235

Splendidly sited by the café and the bridge at Skenfrith, this luxurious 17th-century coaching inn serves fine cuisine sourced 'from as many local farms and suppliers as possible'. Main courses might include fillet of Brecon beef or glazed breast of local duck. The food is complemented by a good wine list and real ales, including Freeminer and Hook Norton, and Broome Farm local scrumpy cider.

Castle View Hotel

Bridge Street, Chepstow, NP16 5EZ
Tel: 01291 620349;
www.hotelchepstow.co.uk

A 300-year-old, ivy-clad, whitewashed pub looking across to the castle and the River Wye. Superb cuisine showcases British specialities with local produce including steaks, and salmon caught from the Wye. There's a charming small beer garden.

King Arthur Hotel

Higher Green, Reynoldston,
Gower, SA3 1AD
Tel: 01792 390775
www.kingarthurhotel.co.uk

Set back from the large village green, the King Arthur Hotel is well-known for its local Welsh dishes including game steaks, pork, laverbread and locally caught fish and cockles. There's a cosy atmosphere with log fires and for summer there's a pleasant garden.

USEFUL NUMBERS

Brecon Beacons National Park Visitors/Mountain Centre
Libanus, Brecon, Powys
Tel: 01874 623366

The Gower Society
Swansea Museum, Victoria Road, Swansea.
www.gowersociety.welshnet.co.uk

Pembrokeshire National Park Centre
The Grove, St David's.
Tel: 01437 720099

Snowdonia National Park Authority
Penrhyndeudraeth, Gwynedd
Tel: 01766 770274

Visit Wales Centre
Tel: 08708 300 306;
www.visitwales.co.uk

ANGLING

Visit Wales publish a free brochure with a list of tackle shops and places to fish, available from TICs or from
www.fishing.visitwales.com

CYCLING

Visit Wales publish a free brochure, available from TICs or their website
www.cycling.visitwales.com
A National cycle network, including a trans-Wales route from Chepstow to Holyhead, Lon Las Cymru, is operated by Sustrans National Cycle Network.
Tel: 0117 926 8893;
www.sustrans.org.uk

WALKING

Visit Wales
www.walking.visitwales.comNational Long Distance Paths

The Cambrian Way
A 275-mile (444km) route over the Brecon Beacons, Mid Wales and Snowdonia.

Offa's Dyke Path
A 170-mile (274km) route from Chepstow to Prestatyn.

Glyndwr's Way
A 132-mile (212km) route through Mid-Wales.

Pembrokeshire Coast Path
A 186-mile coastal route from Tenby to St Dogmaels.

WALKERS' EVENTS
Gower Walking Festival
Early Jun. Tel: 01792 361302
Anglesey Walking Festival
Mid Jun. Tel: 01248 725700
Conwy's Walking Festival
Mid-late Jul.
www.conwy.gov.uk/countryside
Barmouth Walking Festival
Mid Sep. Tel: 01341 281565
International 4-day Walks
Mid-Sep. Llanwrtyd Wells.
Tel: 01591 610666

VISITORS WITH DISABILITIES

Disabilities Wales
Tel: 029 20887325;
www.disabilitywales.org

INDEX

INDEX

ACKNOWLEDGEMENTS

The Automobile Association would like to thank the following photographers, companies and picture libraries for their assistance in the preparation of this book.

Abbreviations for the picture credits are as follows – (t) top; (b) bottom; (c) centre; (l) left; (r) right; (AA) AA World Travel Library.

2/3 AA/N Jenkins; 5 AA/G Matthews; 6 AA/N Jenkins; 9 AA/N Jenkins; 12 AA/C&A Molyneux; 13t AA/P Aithie; 13b AA/P Aithie; 14l AA/G Matthews; 14r AA/N Jenkins; 15t AA/G Matthews; 15b AA/G Matthews; 16 AA/N Jenkins; 17 AA/R Eames; 19 AA/I Burgum; 20 AA/N Jenkins; 23 AA/I Burgum; 24 AA; 26 AA/P Aithie; 28/29 AA/G Matthews; 30 AA/G Matthews; 31 AA/N Jenkins; 32 AA/P Aithie; 33 AA/P Aithie; 34 AA; 37 AA/S Watkins; 38/39 AA/N Jenkins; 43 AA/S Watkins; 44 AA/A Grierley; 47 AA/G Matthews; 48 AA/P Aithie; 55 AA/G Munday; 56 AA/I Burgum; 58 AA/S Watkins; 60/61 AA/S Watkins; 62 AA/S Watkins; 63 AA/N Jenkins; 64t AA/D Croucher; 64b AA/C Jones; 65l AA/R Newton; 65r AA/N Jenkins; 66 AA/R Newton; 70 AA/R Eames; 73 AA/P Davies; 74 AA/R Newton; 77 AA/R Newton; 78/79 AA/N Jenkins; 82 AA/R Eames; 85 AA/G Matthews; 86/87 AA/H Williams; 89 AA/S Watkins; 90/91 AA/S Watkins; 92 AA/G Matthews; 99 AA/S Watkins; 100 AA/N Jenkins; 102 AA; 104/105 AA/I Burgum; 106 AA/R Newton; 107t AA/N Jenkins; 107b AA/C Jones; 108 AA/N Jenkins; 108/109 AA/G Matthews; 110 AA/D Croucher; 113 AA/N Jenkins; 114/115 AA/I Burgum; 117 AA/I Burgum; 119 AA; 120/121 AA/C Jones; 122/123 AA/I Burgum; 124 AA/N Jenkins; 126 AA/N Jenkins; 135 AA/C Jones; 136 AA/R Newton; 138 AA/R Eames; 140/141 AA/N Jenkins; 142 AA/I Burgum; 143 AA/C Molyneux; 144t AA/D Croucher; 144b AA/M Allwood-Coppin; 145 AA/C&A Molyneux; 146/147 AA/N Jenkins; 150/151 AA/N Jenkins; 153 AA/N Jenkins; 154 156 AA/N Jenkins; 159 AA/V Bates; 162/163 AA/C&A Molyneux; 165 AA/C Molyneux; 171 AA/I Burgum; 172 AA/N Jenkins; 174 AA/H Williams; 176/177 AA/M Moody; 178 AA/M Allwood-Coppin; 179t AA/N Jenkins; 179b AA/C Molyneux; 180 AA/C Molyneux; 181 AA/C Molyneux; 182 AA/C Molyneux; 186 AA/N Jenkins; 189 AA/I Burgum; 190/191 AA/N Jenkins; 195 AA/N Jenkins; 196 AA/M Moody; 198/199 AA/M Moody; 201 AA/N Jenkins; 207 AA/M Moody; 208 AA/N Jenkins; 210 AA; 212/213 214 AA/N Jenkins; 215 AA/N Jenkins; 216t AA/I Burgum; 216b AA/I Burgum; 217 AA/N Jenkins; 219 AA/N Jenkins; 221 AA/J Gravell; 222 AA/G Matthews; 224 AA/N Jenkins; 226/227 AA/N Jenkins; 229 230 AA/I Burgum; 232 AA/N Jenkins; 234/235 AA/M Moody; 237 AA/C Jones; 238/239 AA; 240/241 AA/I Burgum; 247 AA/I Burgum; 248 AA/N Jenkins.

Every effort has been made to trace the copyright holders, and we apologise in advance for any accidental errors. We would be happy to apply the corrections in the following edition of this publication.